# CAREER EDUCATION for TEACHERS and COUNSELORS: A practical approach

# CAREER EDUCATION for TEACHERS and COUNSELORS:
# A practical approach

**LARRY J. BAILEY**
*Professor, College of Education,*
*Southern Illinois University*
*at Carbondale*

*Foreword by*
DAVID V. TIEDEMAN
International College,
Guild of Tutors

Second Edition

THE CARROLL PRESS
*Publishers*
43 Squantum Street
Cranston, R.I. 02920

*About the Author*

**LARRY J. BAILEY** is a Professor of Vocational Education Studies at Southern Illinois University in Carbondale. Dr. Bailey completed the doctoral degree at the University of Illinois in 1968. He was on the faculty at the University of Illinois and the University of Iowa prior to joining Southern Illinois University.

He has served as a member of the National Advisory Council for Career Education, the National Advisory Board for the ERIC Clearinghouse in Career Education, and the Advisory Council on Adult, Vocational and Technical Education, State of Illinois.

Dr. Bailey is the author of more than 100 articles, books, book chapters, research reports and miscellaneous publications.

©   Copyright 1973 by McKnight Publishing Company under title *Career Education: New Approaches to Human Development* by Larry J. Bailey and Ronald Stadt.

©   Copyright 1985 by Larry J. Bailey.

**Library of Congress Cataloging in Publication Data**

Bailey, Larry J.
    Career education for teachers and counselors.

    Rev. ed. of: Career education. 1973.
    Includes bibliographies and index.
    1. Career education — United States. 2. Vocational guidance of women — United States. I. Bailey, Larry J. Career education. II. Title.

*LC1037.5.B3*     *1985*     *370.11'3*     *85-13959*
    *ISBN 0-910328-41-2 (paperback)*

Manufactured in the United States of America

# DEDICATION

*To Tad and Vernon who taught me how to work.*

# CONTENTS

# CONTENTS – *Continued*

# LIST OF ILLUSTRATIONS

# FOREWORD

---

We humans can know the joy of accomplishment – if we work at something in full integrity, that is. Thoughts of accomplishments come to us humans all the time. More come to us when we are open than when we are anxious. We also enjoy the capacity to choose among our thoughts, to know some of their effects, and to change our minds about what we want and what we are getting. And, most miraculous of all, our accomplishments which are good for both universe and us invariably manifest to our glory and to everything's glory. "Both/and" proves to be one after all when we are in the right universe relationship.

At 65, I know the joy of accomplishment in my work career which I focused upon the study of career. Thanks to Dr. Anna Miller-Tiedeman, my study of career has brought us together into accommodation of life-as-career, or LIFECAREER as we both abbreviate life-as-career and uniquely denote it so all will know it as the pathing in life process, not just as the job condition in which "career" is now rather commonly taken solely to be.

Appreciation of life-as-career did not spring as Minerva fully blown from my Jupiter's forehead. I had to labor for my present appreciation of life-as-career. In my labor, I witnessed, and somewhat empowered, the metamorphosis of: (1) occupational success into occupational choice in the 1940's; (2) occupational choice into vocational development in the 1950's; (3) vocational development into career development in the 1960's; (4) career development into career education in the 1970's; and, hopefully, will also witness (5) the metamorphosis of career education into lifecareering in the 1980's. I think such will actually happen because social conditions are now propitious for such a turn.

xiii

It is from such an evolving lifecareer context that I first be-friended and began to learn from my former Illinois colleague, Professor Larry J. Bailey. Professor Bailey climbed aboard the transition from career development to career education when that transition started in the early 1970's. Bailey subsequently peered sufficiently deeply into the personal career to know that its education must have harmony with its development, must illuminate and enable forward possibilities, and must stem from personal integration of play and work within the lifecareer process. In this part of his own lifecareer, Bailey has done seminal work on the differentiation of work from play in children. In addition, the developmental curriculum model which he presents in Chapter Four holds promise towards the initial re-integration of that differentiating condition of play and work for the individual. If such differentiation and re-integration can occur, and can be apprehended as well in its occurrences, United States citizens will emerge as masters of their lifecareers. Hooray! That's a greatly to be desired outcome of career education.

With such interests and work, it was natural that Professor Bailey would play a leading role in bringing career to the fore in American education beginning in 1970 in association with what was then the U.S. Office of Education. Bailey first served as re-searcher in career education, then as state leader in the infusion of career education into elementary and secondary schools, next as national advisor concerning both library access to career education resources and the nationalization of career education in our schools while all the time also continually serving as teacher and writer con-cerning the career education process. Bailey has truly carved out a distinguished unfolding of his career in his fifteen-year concern with career education.

This book clearly gives you the advantage of what Dr. Miller-Tiedeman (in her new book, *How to Not Make It − and Succeed: The Truth about Your LIFECAREER*) calls a personal career com-pass − one's experience, intuition, and intelligence − at play in the general career education process. Bailey's career compass for this book comes out of his research and public service as well as from a previous, large volume, *Career Education: New Approaches to Human Development*, which Bailey did with his colleague, Professor Ronald Stadt over a decade ago. This present, modern and refined volume, *Career Education for Teachers and Counselors: A Practical Approach,* not only now has the depth and breadth of Bailey's fifteen years of work in career education, it also has an exquisite timeliness about it. The recent federal presence in career education has, for all practical purposes, now fully dissipated. Thus today it remains to be seen whether state and local school systems and/or individual teachers and counselors continue the initiative in career education or not. Professor Bailey and I both hope that they do.

Professor Bailey's and my hopes for the continuation of career education throughout the United States are manifest in this book. You will find that Bailey has mercifully cut the book down to five-chapter size. Each of his chapters considers an important part of the fuller process of living life-as-career and, therefore, each deserves your careful study.

Chapter One sets the social context within which attention to career emerged as a solution both for the nation's economic transitions at play in the seventies and eighties and the continuing evolution of consciousness through the human career. Unfortunately, politicians of education mostly consider just the former of these two purposes. But citizens educated beyond schooling in life-as-career consider both purposes while emphasizing the latter because it stems primarily from individual attention. Citizens so educated can thus eventually know life-as-career as their own self-organizing system.

Chapter Two deals with the manner in which federal leadership emerged in politically solving some of the country's economic problems. Fortunately, Constitutional silence on direct federal involvement in education made the career education initiative one which had to be shared with the state and local school systems, not imposed upon them by their federation. Career education as a national initiative, therefore, had to be accomplished by personal choices and the education of educational professionals themselves, not by prescriptive federal fiat. This fortuitous circumstance permits career education to embrace self-organizing system theory unequivocally when educators understand transformation in consciousness sufficiently to appreciate its power and to empower others in such understandings of this life-as-career process in its generality.

Women as well as minorities became acutely aware of individually operating in their self-organizing systems (which are their own lives-as-careers) during the federal career education era. Bailey devotes Chapter Three to women's issues in work career. However, as a career educator, you should not consider mastery of self-organizing system theory in living life-as-career to be just a female matter. In fact, self-organizing system theory works regardless of age, race, creed, color, gender, or ethnicity because universe is itself a self-organizing system. Universe's self-organizing system operation, therefore, always figures in the full operation of persons as universe microcosms. Our Constitution honors this realization in figuratively offering simple justice to all. But the practical problem with our Constitution is human beings themselves. For instance, it took us humans two centuries to begin treating blacks with simple justice in the United States. And women in western societies suffered an even longer denial of simple justice in their lifecareers.

Bailey gets into the bread and butter of career education in Chapter Four — doing career education itself. And he does so in his usual comprehensive way. He presents a model of six outcome types which are to be attended to in each of four stages throughout elementary and secondary schooling. This Bailey model has always interested me. For instance, its six types of developmental outcomes make sense. Furthermore, its implicit realization that physical and cognitive capacities develop in elementary and secondary schooling and demand staging in a general way also makes sense. Finally, Bailey's teaching of teachers and counselors how to use such a general concept in organized fashion during schooling makes sense as well. But what Bailey fails to register concerning his model is that you have to present both the forest and the trees of its outcomes and stages when you begin to teach and counsel from the model. Otherwise, you will begin to teach and counsel by the book rather than by personal understanding of the condition you wish to empower your students to be in. When you do things by the book rather than by understanding, things taught become so seemingly complicated that understanding and appreciation seldom ensue in those you seek to help. However, when you teach and counsel in order to give people both a perceptual sense of some whole which is in them, and to find expression of that whole in relation to what you ask them to do, you facilitate their accommodation of the whole because you have helped them to go in as well as to come out more. And this personal work on and by the self is far different from just administering some "self concept measure" to students and merely laying its language upon them. In fact, you then find yourself helping your students focus upon the personal act of conceptualizing that which is presumably known to another. And in this process your students will empower themselves in that which is known to another and in how they themselves get to know. You will then have taught them to *fish* in *life-as-process* rather than just given them a "job fish" in that process which is known to you but which is still unfathomable to them.

Bailey's command of curriculum construction and teaching shows fully in Chapter Five. This chapter teaches you how to construct, implement, and evaluate lesson plans in career education. And it does so well. However, keep looking for the forest of life-as-career process as you get into the trees of this chapter as well. The forest of career education ought to be the eventual student mastery of life-as-career process. I honestly don't know how far mastery of life-as-career process can develop in elementary and secondary school.

However, I do know that life-as-career process is always developing, and starts at birth. Therefore, something is going on and discerning teachers and counselors can apprehend what is transpiring.

Keep yourselves open to mastery of the life-as-career process as you career educate with the foundations of career education provided in this book. I hope you personally aspire to understanding that spiritual process which inheres in life-as-career. It's in you waiting to come out. Let it out. And lifecareer joyfully as you inform your intelligence by this book as well as by your intuition and thus enlarge your experience through direct participation in career education. Such action will further perfect your own career compass — your experience, intuition, and intelligence.

By all means, be fully human in your mastery of this book. You will then know the joy of accomplishment in career education which will materialize in your evolving understanding with guidance from this work.

DAVID V. TIEDEMAN
International College
Guild of Tutors

*Los Angeles, California*
*April, 1985*

# PREFACE

In 1973, a book by Professor Ronald Stadt and me was published by McKnight Publishing Company entitled *Career Education: New Approaches to Human Development.* It was written because of our perception of the need for a comprehensive text and reference book dealing with the social, historical, theoretical, philosophical and psychological foundations of career education. We did not direct the book toward a specific clientele, intending rather that it be used by a wide range of students, practitioners and other education professionals.

Another need exists in 1985, but now for a new type of book written especially for the practitioner. An introductory text is required that can be used at both the preservice and inservice levels, and perhaps the graduate level as well. Specific, intended uses for this book are:

1. As an undergraduate text for a two or three semester hour career education course for preservice education majors.

2. As an inservice text for teachers, counselors, administrators and other school personnel.

3. As a supplemental text in other types of education courses such as: elementary education, secondary education, special education, counselor education, educational administration, vocational and practical arts education, curriculum and instruction, teaching methods, and evaluation.

4. As a basic text at the graduate level if augmented by related topics and additional readings.

Three chapters of this book are revisions from the 1973 text, and two chapters are new. Chapter One entitled "The Climate for Change" is a shortened version of combined Chapters One and Two of the first book. Chapter Two on "The Career Education Movement" is essentially new although it incorporates short sections from the earlier Chapter Eight. The "Career Development Needs of Women", Chapter Three, is an updated and revised chapter based on Chapter Three in Bailey and Stadt. Chapter 11 in the old book was revised to become the new Chapter Four, "A Developmental Curriculum Model for Career Education". The last chapter "Planning, Implementing and Evaluating Career Education" is new. The Appendices extend concepts and methods explained in Chapter Five.

A debt of gratitude is owed the following three individuals for their direct and indirect contributions to this book: To my colleague, Ronald W. Stadt, for allowing me to adapt for Chapter One two chapters he originally wrote for our earlier text; to Henry P. Cole of the University of Kentucky for permission to include his seven "Qualities for Career Education Curricula" in Chapter Five; and, to Sidney C. High, Jr. (now retired) formerly of the federal Office of Career Education for so generously sharing resource materials and for his other numerous comments and suggestions.

LARRY J. BAILEY

*Carbondale, Illinois*
*February, 1985*

*Chapter One*

# 1

## THE CLIMATE FOR CHANGE

---

### Introduction

On January 23, 1971 then Commissioner of Education, Sidney P. Marland, Jr. walked on a convention platform in Houston, Texas and delivered his famous "Career Education Now"[1] speech.* Even though the goal of learning about and preparing for work has been advocated throughout the long history of formal education, the speech caught many within the education profession off-guard. Partly because the speech was Marland's first major address as commissioner, and partly because of a tendency to view the federal role in education with suspicion, some people dismissed the proposal as another ill-conceived fad emanating from the U.S. Office of Education.

Marland, however, was a competent and experienced educational administrator who was sensitive to criticisms of education and mindful of the need to reform the nature and substance of learning. The purpose of this chapter is to review statements made by education critics during the years immediately preceding the Marland speech to demonstrate the educational and social climates in existence at that time. The review is intended to illuminate why career education evolved in the early 1970s as a response to demands for educational reform.[2]

### Contemporary Educational Criticism

The launch of Sputnik I by the Soviet Union in October 1957 provided a catharsis and set in motion an era that Postman and Wein-gartner[3] called the "contemporary era of school criticism." They further identified three sub-periods within the era they called *Panic*

---

* The speech will be discussed in detail in Chapter Two.

1

*Phase I* (1957-60), the *Romantic Phase* (1960-1970), and *Panic Phase II* (early 1970s). Educational criticism during this era evolved half-cycle from reactionary (late 1950s) to revolutionary (early 1970s). This chapter will deal with educational criticism only during the latter part of the era.

A gross categorization of types of criticism, adapted from McNally and Passow,[4] serves as an outline for this chapter as follows: (a) concern for individuals and equal educational opportunity, (b) concern for important learnings, and (c) concern for the structure of schooling and school-society relationships. Lest this become a book dealing only with educational criticism, only some of the major critics are treated under each category.

## Concern for Individuals and Equal Educational Opportunity

There is ample evidence to support the contention that concern for individual human beings was at the base of nearly all *Romantic Phase* and *Panic Phase II* educational criticism. Beginning in the mid-1960s, there were many cogent arguments advanced for schooling which is vastly more humanizing than the jailhouse existence to which millions of young are subjected 180 or so days a year. Prominent among these treatises was *Education and Ecstasy* by Leonard.[5] Leonard maintained that education, at its best, is ecstatic. "When joy is absent, the effectiveness of the learning process falls and falls until the human being is operating hesitantly, grudgingly, fearfully at only a tiny fraction of his potential".[6] Leonard laid out very good arguments for the learning potential of individuals, for technology, and for their combination in schools which are the natural extension of successful educational enterprises. After noting that credentials are screening devices used by employers who do not care what people have learned but only that they have survived the system, Leonard dismissed the teaching of traditional subjects such as English after grade seven. He seemed pleased that schools fail in their present task which is ". . . to teach a few tricks and otherwise limit possibilities, narrow perceptions and bring the individual's career as a learner (changer) to an end"[7]. On the premises that highly interactive and regenerative technology requires mass genius, mass creativity and life-long learning, and that " . . . schools as they now exist are already obsolete"[8], Leonard described a very exciting and humanizing education, showing throughout that:

1. The human potential is infinitely greater than we have been led to believe.

2. Learning is sheer delight.

3. Learning itself is life's ultimate purpose[9]

Leonard was very familiar with the literature of educational criticism and quick to illustrate that Conant[10] was remiss to assume that the structure of schooling was a "given." The open and highly mechanized school Leonard prophesied would entail new school-society relationships. Students and parents would come and go as they please, participating in varied experiences when and for as long as they wish. In a real sense, *Education and Ecstasy* was a fetching argument for the kinds of learning advocated in this book.

Another poignant reappraisal of traditional classroom conduct and a brilliant suggestion for reform on behalf of student welfare and creativity was *Teaching as a Subversive Activity*.[11] Because of its style, this book should be read in its entirety to be appreciated. It is filled with item-by-item suggestions for conducting discussions which permit young people to develop rather than be stifled. Suffice it here to cite five suggestions which Postman and Weingartner submitted which were acceptable to teachers whom they had in classes.

1. Eliminate all conventional "tests" and "testing."

2. Eliminate all "courses."

3. Eliminate all "requirements."

4. Eliminate all full-time administrators and administrations.

5. Eliminate all restrictions that confine learners to sitting still in boxes inside of boxes.[12]

One can see that individualized education, different from the vogue in many ways, would remain.

Much of the concern for education to be more personalized came together with the larger concern for alleviating urban and rural poverty and consequent disadvantages in employment, education, housing and other conditions. Many of the people who managed government programs for disadvantaged individuals in the 1960s challenged traditional definitions of the form and function of education. One of the more coherent presentations regarding meaningful learning for youth from poverty areas was *On the Outskirts of Hope* by Dawson.[13] Dawson described an unorthodox approach to reaching the disassociated. She contended that success depends upon (a) awareness of the problems of the poverty stricken, of historical attitudes toward ethnic groups, and of living conditions in the ghetto; (b) teachers and educational administrators who foster innovation and service and are not shocked by atypical behavior; (c) learning experiences which are not restricted by walls, established course outlines, and preconceived notions about appropriate behavior patterns;

(d) instructional techniques which are more like those used by clinicians than those used by authoritarian teachers; and (e) evaluative techniques which demonstrate learning successes and simulate employment tests. Dawson's suggestions should be taken in light of the fact that they stemmed from her personal successes during three years of teaching Manpower Development and Training Act (MDTA) students in San Francisco. Too few theoreticians have this base of experience.

Clark[14] was one of the more articulate spokespersons for better education in ghettos. He deemed contemporary education to be very inadequate.

> ... The present level of public school inefficiency has reached an intolerable stage of public calamity. It must be demonstrated that minority group children are not the only victims of the monopolistic inefficiency of the present pattern of organization and functioning of our public schools.
> It must be demonstrated that white children — privileged white children whose parents understandably seek to protect them by moving to suburbs or by sending them to private and parochial schools — also suffer both potentially and immediately.
> It must be demonstrated that business and industry suffer intolerable financial burdens of double and triple taxation in seeking to maintain a stable economy in the face of the public school inefficiency which produces human casualties rather than constructive human beings.
> It must be demonstrated that the cost in correctional, welfare, and health services is intolerably high in seeking to cope with consequences of educational inefficiency — that it would be more economical, even for an affluent society, to pay the price and meet the demands of efficient public education.
> It must be demonstrated that a nation which presents itself to the world as the guardian of democracy and the protector of human values throughout the world cannot itself make a mockery of these significant ethical principles by dooming one-tenth of its own population to a lifetime of inhumane futility because of remediable educational deficiencies in its public schools.[15]

Another prominent appeal to reorient schooling was Glasser's[16] *Schools Without Failure.* Glasser is a psychiatrist who had experience with ghetto peoples in correctional institutions. In keeping with many other critics, he submitted that schooling was failure-oriented. He proposed that his theory of reality therapy be applied in schools. This would mean increased involvement, relevance, and thinking at the expense of memory and drill. Schools should be changed so that responsibility and success would replace failure and the tendency toward withdrawal and delinquency.

Among Glasser's proposals was elimination of punishment, the development of discipline in individuals, progression from small successes to larger ones, no excuses from responsibility, and positive involvement. He advocated classroom group counseling, led by the teacher. Daily time devoted to developing social responsibility would be necessary to solving behavioral and educational problems of people who evidence the negative effects of poverty and bad social conditions. Glasser's successes in correctional education were reflected in detailed proposals regarding testing, heterogeneous classes, homework, and student classification. In keeping with some of the more successful ghetto community colleges, he proposed a grading system which reports success and eliminates failure labels.

Glasser's was a very simple, logical, and realizable proposal for taking disadvantaged and delinquent or potentially delinquent youngsters, meeting them more than half way with love and the promise of forgiving past but not future misbehavior, introducing learning successes, and building on these successes. *Schools Without Failure* developed the very compelling realization that procedures for moving misbehaving young people to reliable and mature, healthy and learning, and sociable and proud people are not only convincingly tempting but already tested and proven in a variety of educational settings from kindergarten to graduate school. In the main, this was an appeal for respecting people and orienting schooling toward individuals instead of toward subject-matter and shallow establishment goals. "All students must be accepted as potentially capable, not as handicapped by their environment".[17]

In a book entitled *Human Teaching for Human Learning,* Brown[18] described the results of an experiment, and the theory behind experiences, which teachers at all levels can use to foster self-awareness. To promote *affective education,* Brown worked regularly with teachers to plan and evaluate experiences which couple intellectual, and emotional, and spiritual learning. Brown submitted that the conference of these learnings can assure relevance without revolution. His book was typical of many which emphasize refocusing on individuals.

There were a great many positive responses to concern for the development of several facets of individuals. Many in-school and perhaps as many out-of-school education programs focused on personal growth. These and a great many more articles and books in the contemporary literature of educational criticism made proposals such as: (a) psychological education for long-term life changes at the expense of short-term subject-matter gains, (b) experiences which develop understanding of fantasies, (c) exploration of the effect of emotions on behavior, (d) sensitizing experiences such as meditations, improvisations, and expressive dance, (e) elimination of harmful habits via self-understanding and living highly active and full existences, (f)

6 Career Education for Teachers and Counselors

challenging experiences, such as Outward Bound, which tax individual physical and emotional strengths, (g) group counseling via seminars and practicums, (h) experience with resolving confrontation and conflict, and (i) open education. The literature of *psychological education* or *affective education* or *education for self-awareness and development* — whatever it may come to be called — is voluminous, fascinating, and not to be taken lightly.

By the end of the 1960s forces were already well-collected for marrying education and psychology to assure the welfare of the individual in a world with man-woman, ghetto-suburb, work-play, and many other increasingly intense relationships. It became apparent that the marriage could be accomplished through experiences which are liberalizing, not only in the sense formerly espoused by classicists who advocated intimate familiarity with the great books, but in the sense personified by Carl Rogers and other behavioral scientists. Put another way, critics were demanding (and schools were beginning to provide) experience modes which foster human growth and understanding. The trend was toward focusing on human problems as dominant and on material problems *and* organized content from the disciplines as secondary. The reader is encouraged to become familiar with the literature of psychological education. It would be well to begin with Part Four of Purpel and Belanger[19] and with *Open Education and the American School* by Barth.[20]

## Concern for Important Learnings

A second major type of criticism had to do with questioning what the schools regarded as important for students to learn. "The overemphasis of abstract knowledge and deemphasis of the arts of the practical have left the curriculum reform movement open to justifiable charges of social and moral irresponsibility."[21] Prior to World War II, a great many influential people advocated schooling at the secondary level consisting almost exclusively of theoretical disciplines. By 1970, however, there were few remaining critics of education who submitted coldly that curriculum should consist of organized disciplines alone.

Martin[22] treated the organized disciplines issue very adequately. In curriculum theory, the disciplines principle of content selection functions together with the principles of structure and inquiry and becomes "teach the structure of the disciplines as inquiry".[23] There is a tendency to call all school subjects or those which one likes "disciplines." This must be avoided. The discipline principle is too limiting because it rules out the teaching of such things as foreign language, art, physical education, and typing. Thus, it is not an acceptable principle by itself. It is better to select subject matter from the disciplines than to select only subjects which are disciplines. Put another way, ". . . education ought not misunderstand or distort the disciplines . . ." and " . . . advocates of the disciplines ought not be allowed to misunderstand or distort education."[24]

Concern for important learnings is better understood by analysis of the meanings of knowledge in curriculum. Lamm[25] identified three formulae: "(a) Knowledge is meant for use. (b) Knowledge has intrinsic value. (c) Knowledge is a means in the process of individuation." According to the first formula, individuals can function acceptably only if they have specified understandings and values. Validity of knowledge is determined by utility. Knowledge permits imitation of a behavioral mode.

The second formula, which holds that knowledge has intrinsic value, is important to advocates of education for acculturation. Transition from one society or culture to another is acculturation. Many educators are concerned with "cross-cultural" approaches to educating various groups. Knowledge is the product of the most "human of human beings" and the means for transforming people into human beings. Knowledge has no value beyond cultivation of human qualities; this is knowledge for its own sake.

Lamm submitted very convincingly that these two approaches to defining important learnings have a common denominator. Both see instruction as a bridge between knowledge and the learner; instruction mediates between knowledge and the learner. Knowledge is laws and models of behavior, and learners lack discipline until they have knowledge. Because of this common denominator, most schools use both the disciplinary and the instrumental approach to instruction. Internalization and conditioning are thought to be justified because the learner has voids.

The third approach to defining important knowledge is the formula: "Knowledge is a means in the process of individuation."[26] This approach assumes that the structure, the form and the substance of knowledge can and should be manipulated and that the learner cannot and should not be manipulated. Adoption of this formula would make a big difference.

Instead of acculturating or manipulating students, schools would be concerned with development of the self-concept and with self-actualization. Lamm was beautifully clear on the implications of this concept of the relationship of knowledge, individuals and schooling.

> . . . We do not learn humanity by acquiring social roles or by internalizing the principles, values, and norms of a specific culture. Humanity is a given datum present in human beings, and education is the process designed to

enable the individual to actualize his own humanity, which is unique to
him as an individual different from others. We thus arrive at a further
assumption. The imparting of knowledge whether as a means of socialization or as a means of acculturation is a process designed to make people
alike (or at least to mold them according to patterns of given social roles
or cultural groups). Society with its patterns and mechanisms and culture
with its values and norms are designed to serve as common denominators
for individuals who are different from one another. The differences among
people make it necessary to adapt the means of imparting knowledge, but
as far as ends are concerned, all people are considered equal. Knowledge
must be imparted differently to gifted children than to ordinary children,
but the role which it is expected to play is the same for both. In this sense,
the difference between people is something which has to be overcome in
order to include everyone in the common denominator which is given in
society (according to those whose end is socialization) or in culture (according to those whose end is acculturation).

According to the radical conception of education, diversity is not an
obstacle to be overcome but a basic premise defining the humanity of
human beings.[27]

Lamm's treatment of creativity, subjectivity, self-awareness, self-reg-
ulation, motivation and other characteristics of the kind of schooling
which views knowledge as a resource for individuals rather than as a
means to molding uncommon novices into common citizens was suc-
cinct and prophetic.

Other writers also began to define important learnings in a way
compatible with development. Gattegno[28] supported the notion that
knowledge is not something which exists prior to learning. Rather,
knowledge should be a consequence of learning. Learning, not teaching, should be the concern of schooling. Gattegno's thesis was that
because children have eyes, professionals should aid and abet their
seeing by clearing out the rubbish and pointing them in the right
direction. This is in contrast to blindfolding children and requiring
them to memorize outdated information about the world.

Purpel and Belanger submitted that because of curriculum projects in the physical sciences ". . . the concept of knowledge has been
updated, away from the conceptualization of knowledge as a finished
product isolated from any human activity and toward a view of
knowledge as open and continually subject to human reinterpreta-
tion and reinvention".[29] Given this new concept of knowledge,
schools would be able to respond to the third category of criticism.

## Concern for the Structure of Schooling and
## School-Society Relationships

A number of very positive suggestions for changing the structure of classroom activities have resulted from practices perfected in

selected schools in the United Kingdom. One major voice in this regard was Featherstone. In *Schools Where Children Learn*, Featherstone[30] reprinted a series of pioneering articles and afterthoughts about teaching. His suggestions were very specific and included descriptions of the following characteristics of *infant schools* in the United Kingdom: (a) use of a great quantity and variety of materials, (b) emphasis on concrete experiences, (c) great reduction of role learning, (d) effective utilization of all manner of building areas and grounds, (e) multiple activities moment-to-moment, (f) socio-psychological climates of cooperation and friendliness, and (g) emphasis on resource allocation rather than instruction and discipline. Featherstone's proposal was hidden from some observers by the level of detail of his descriptions. The scope of his proposal is clearest when the reader considers the mature teacher's responsibility in the infant school. Professionalism becomes a measurable matter. The quality of relationship established with individuals in a doctor-client kind of setting determines, in large part, the effectiveness of educational experiences. Focus on children and the process of learning, and changes in the physical and organizational structure of the education enterprise, are basic.

A professional colleague recently discussed curriculum reform with the staff of an infant school outside Birmingham. According to him, these teachers would not consider a carefully patterned curriculum and were quick to supply advantages (always from the children's view) of the freer methods and environment over traditional schools. Although they appreciated the fundamental and far-reaching contrasts between open and traditional primary schooling, they underscored the ease of modification to, and conduct of, child-centered curricula.

One of the major contributors to the practice and literature of "open" or "free schooling" in America was Kohl. In *The Open Classroom,* Kohl[31] drew generalizations from observations made in his own teaching and consulting. He was quick to condemn American education as consisting, for most children, of one authoritarian and oppressive system. Everywhere the teacher's foremost concern is to establish and maintain discipline. Only in the best schools are there genuine attempts to cover planned curricula. In these, rigid sequences are boring, degrading, and misguided. Kohl proposed the open classroom because children's learning is episodic rather than vertical or linear. Working together in an open classroom means responding to expressed interests and moving freely in the community. Kohl gave many practical suggestions for working within the existing structure of physical facilities, required textbooks, grading, and reporting. At base, it was the structure of authority and prescription that Kohl challenged. Like Featherstone and many others, Kohl spoke for a new student-professional relationship and introduced the concept of community education which is treated later in this section.

One of the monuments of educational criticism was Silberman's[32] *Crisis in the Classroom.* Silberman advocated alleviation of what he calls "Education for Docility." Several kinds of criticisms of schools, including the concept that schools should be eliminated, have persisted over several centuries because of characteristics which are displayed by nearly all schools. As described by Silberman, these are:

1.  Compulsion. By law or by parental insistence, American children must be in school.

2.  Duration. Five or six hours a day, five days a week, thirty or forty weeks a year, for twelve or more years.

3.  Collective experience. Economy of scale requires a crowd.

4.  Evaluation. Constant assessment differentiates power and authority between student and teacher.

From classroom visits by himself and his staff during the "Carnegie Study" and from the literature of educatonal criticism, Silberman cited many items and incidents which supported the contentions (a) that these characteristics are ubiquitous over time and place, and (b) that they impede learning and foster docility. Silberman also demonstrated the failures of team teaching, instructional television, ungraded or nongraded primaries, massive curriculum projects which were accelerated by Sputnik, and generally irrelevant content. He laid a great deal of the failure at the feet of reformers who were unaware that their proposals had been made by theorists in the 1920s and 1930s.

Silberman treated innovations in educational technology with the same keen analysis that he applied to curriculum reform. He is to be respected for not condemning good features. He was strong in pointing out (a) that reform is meaningless if it assumes educational establishment instead of individual goals, and (b) that technology is suspect unless it is under-girded by a thorough theory of teaching. He concluded that the pressing educational problem ". . . is not how to increase the efficiency of the schools; it is how to create and maintain a humane society. A society whose schools are inhumane is not likely to be humane itself."[33] The bulk of *Crisis in the Classroom* was devoted to how schools should be changed. In short, this would entail eliminating unexamined practices.

> The preoccupation with order and control, the slavish adherence to the timetable and lesson plan, the obsession with routine *qua* routine, the absence of noise and movement, the joylessness and repression, the uni-

versality of the formal lecture or teacher-dominated "discussion" in which the teacher instructs an entire class as a unit, the emphasis of the verbal and de-emphasis of the concrete, the inability of students to work on their own, the dichotomy of work and play — none of these are necessary; all can be eliminated.[34]

In a milestone article, "End of the Impossible Dream " Schrag[35] submitted that we should have learned in the 1960s that ". . . there is no magic in the single school system or in any set of curricular prescriptions, and that the most successful motivating device may simply be the sense that one has chosen what he wants to learn and under what conditions." He argued for multiple options and values, i.e., for separate schools, which are accountable to their clients. By "impossible dream," Schrag meant the concept that everyone could be successful by reason of education, i.e., the promise of equality and opportunity. Alluding to statistics regarding dropouts and ethnic groups, he concluded that ". . . nothing in school makes as much difference as the economic background of the student and the social and economic backgrounds of his peers"[36] Perhaps because of simplicity, Schrag more convincingly than most, dismissed the linear standard from bright to slow and the competitive spirit of schooling. More than anything else, schools "certify and legitimize success and failure".[37] "Cash and power . . . can be converted into degrees, then reconverted into more cash and power".[38] Schrag's advocacy of alternate forms of schooling went beyond the recommendations of authors previously cited and foreshadows some that follow.[39] That there should be new relationships between school and society, and basic changes in the form and function of schooling, was a predominant idea.

One of the more manageable proposals for overcoming inadequacies of schoolhouse education was made by Kerensky and Melby..[40] In *Education II: The Social Imperative,* they analyzed the inadequacies of schools in much the same fashion as critics already noted and proposed actions which alter school-community relationships. They cited Schrag and Silberman, showing similarities and agreeing that schools are the final destructive forces for many children. The gist of the underlying argument for *Education II* is paraphrased as follows:

1.  Even if pressent schools could be successful with poor, black and rural youth, education acquired in childhood and youth will not be long lasting.

2.  Therefore, educating adults is as important as educating children.

3.  Individuals should review their responsibility and practice participation in their own community.

4.  Thus, schools should be community schools.

5.  Personality development, also emphasis on cognitive learning, utilization of a variety of professional and non-professional instructional personnel, and other, new features are necessary to community schools.[41]

Kerensky and Melby identified two basic characteristics of schoolhouse education, which contribute to its inadequacy. First is the sequence of daily demands, which everyone knows many youngsters will fail. (We have heard this from many other authors.) Educators have responded to failure with more of the same content and technology which have failed to resolve problems in the past. Kerensky and Melby submitted that all individuals have intellect, that each may have an exciting intellect, and that learning can be fun and intellectual. They challenged the following assumptions:

1.  That some children will inevitably fail.

2.  That the schoolroom is the child's entire education.

3.  That knowledge is the end of education.

4.  That present administration and control are satisfactory.

Kerensky and Melby agreed with other authors that schools have failed most with the children of the poor and underscore the fact that awareness of inner city problems has had the advantage of magnifying concern to improve. Again, in concert with many other critics, the authors assess what is known of human growth and development and concluded (a) that educational measurement has fostered elitism, (b) that the new psychology presents a more hopeful view of human growth, (c) that education must involve children and youth and adults in self-actualization, (d) that creativity exists in all children, (e) that teachers must relate to individual children, (f) that all can learn, (g) that no two children are alike, (i) that community education is essential and (j) that school management can achieve change only if it has ". . . .belief in people and assumes the leadership in developing a staff that can take children and adults where they are and assist them in setting and achieving higher aspirations".[42]

The last half of *Education II* described *community education.* According to Kerensky and Melby, community education is essential if all of the children of all of the people are to be educated and if we are to alleviate the present situation, wherein one million inadequately prepared youngsters are dumped on society each year. Community education would have the following features:

1.  Leaders who think not only of schools but also of all manner of educational resources in the community. Profession-

als, children, and parents will grow together in the educa-
tion-centered community.

2.  Orientation to subject, or school, or tradition will be re-
    placed by focus on individual children.

3.  Failure will be replaced by reliance on the self-concept and
    new attitudes regarding human potential.

4.  Variability of people will be valued and no method of seg-
    regation will be tolerated.

5.  Marking will be banished and reporting will entail descrip-
    tions of people and their accomplishments.

6.  Schools will be ungraded and individuals will work at ap-
    propriate levels, at their own rates, successfully as they go.

7.  Teachers will seek and be rewarded by the hard tasks.

8.  The class size will depend upon student need.

9.  Teachers will have decision-making power. This will require
    basic organizational change.[43]

*Education II* also suggested forms of school finance, mobilization of
community resources, a more integrated society, and professional
development which are necessary to America's survival. The descriptions and arguments are simple, cogent, and acceptable, especially
because they are realizable.

Few would challenge the statement that Illich[44], [45], [46] was the
extreme, contemporary critic of education. In *The False Ideology of
Schooling* he reviewed a number of criticisms concerning poverty,
equality, international competition, and other such concerns, stating
as have almost all critics of note that in school, the rich win and the
poor lose. As do many other observers, Illich abhorred the belief that
schools can label people correctly for life roles. "School inevitably
gives individuals who . . . dropout, as well as those who don't make it
at all, a rationale for their own inferiority. . . To buy the schooling
hoax is to purchase a ticket for the back seat in a bus headed
nowhere".[47] In *Deschooling Society,* Illich[48] called for a cultural
revolution. After challenging the belief that ever-increasing production, consumption, and profit are measures of the quality of life, he
suggested four guarantees to protect individuals:

1.  The State shall make no law with respect to the establish-
    ment of education. There shall be no ritual obligatory for
    all.

2.  To facilitate disestablishment, there must be a law which
    forbids discrimination in voting, working, and learning.

This would not exclude appropriate performance tests but would prevent favoritism to people who learn skills at the largest public expenditure.

3. The third reform would guarantee each individual equal public educational resources. This would be a generalized GI bill, an "edu-credit card" for each citizen.

4. The fourth legal guarantee would prohibit inquiries into previous school performance. This would protect people from the education monopoly and detach competence judgments from curriculum labels.

Unlike most of the reformers cited thus far, Illich did not go into step-by-step detail regarding reform. He provided only guidelines. For example, in an ideal system ". . . there should be no obstacle for anyone at any time of his life to be able to choose instruction among hundreds of definable skills at public expense".[49] All who want to learn should be provided resources throughout life. Technology can foster independence and learning or bureaucracy and teaching. Technology can be a liberating educational method via (a) reference services to educational objects, (b) skill exchanges, (c) peer matching, and (d) reference services to educators at large. Elsewhere Illich[50] said that the end of schooling may usher in the "global schoolhouse." His proposals were more compatible with contemporary, leading-edge thought in education than most of his many critics were aware. Only his introductory remarks regarding the four approaches to matching students and learning resources are included here.

1. Reference Services to Education Objects — which facilitate access to things or processes used for formal learning. Some of these things can be reserved for this purpose, stored in libraries, rental agencies, laboratories, and showrooms like museums and theaters; others can be in daily use in factories, airports, or on farms, but made available to students as apprentices or on off-hours.

2. Skill Exchanges — which permit persons to list their skills, the conditions under which they are willing to serve as models for others who want to learn these skills, and the addresses at which they can be reached.

3. Peer-Matching — a communications network which permits persons to describe the learning activity in which they wish to engage, in the hope of finding a partner for the inquiry.

4. Reference Services to Educators-at-Large — who can be listed in the directory giving the addresses and self-descriptions of professionals, para-professionals, and free-lancers, along with conditions of access to their services. Such educators, as we will see, could be chosen by polling or consulting their former clients.[51]

Some authors[52] dismiss vast parts of Illich's analysis and suggestions. This writer takes him seriously, especially because he foresaw models and delivery systems in many ways similar to the Office of Education proposals regarding career education models and because he envisions pluralistic educational systems for life, not compartmentalized education. Given careful reading, Illich can be seen to say that it is the monopolistic delivery system, not the essence of schools as institutions, that he challenges. Whereas he would "deschool" society, he would, at the same time, "schools it".

The views of two of the more widely known critics have been saved for last. These are Berg[53] and Goodman.[54, 55] These authors agreed with many of the complaints leveled by other critics and are noted for a special observation. They challenged, with good evidence and logic, commonly held conceptions regarding the relationship of education and employment. Goodman submitted that it is ironic to have schools that estrange students when the function of education in advanced countries is to help each youngster find his or her calling:

> . . . the majority of so-called students in college and high schools do not want to be there and ought not to be. An academic environment is not the appropriate means of education for most young people, including most of the bright.[56]

According to Goodman, because there is strong empirical evidence that schools have little effect on citizenship and vocational ability, because schooling has so many negative results, and because tutelage is against nature and arrests growth, formal schooling should be drastically reduced. From ages six to eleven, children should go to small, neighborhood schools, moving freely from home to school. Education should be incidental.

For adolescents, education should vary. Some should attend college preparatory academies. Some should be supported in apprenticeships, travel, browsing, and self-directed study, research, and programs such as VISTA.

> The belief that a highly industralized society requires twelve to twenty years of prior processing of the young is an illusion or a hoax. The evidence is strong that there is no correlation between school performance and life achievement in any of the professions.[57]

Schooling exists to police the young and to occupy the young unemployed. Thus, youth lobby for free choice by resisting authority. "By multiplying options, it should be possible to find an interesting course for each individual youth, as we now do for only some of the emotionally disturbed and troublemakers".[58] Each must know he is taken seriously as a person.

Goodman condemned the jailhouse existence of schooling, envisaged continuing and community education, and conceived of different delivery systems for preparing people for changing jobs. His ideas unify the less systematic criticisms of schools which are not integral with the larger society. Several of his challenges are worthy of long professional soul-searching and research. For example:

> .. .learning to learn usually means picking up the structure of behavior of the teachers . . . .[59]

> The problem of knowing is to have attentive experience . . . Schools are bad at this. Interesting reality is good.[60]

> . . .I don't agree with the theory of Head Start, that disadvantaged children need special training for their intellectual faculties to prepare them for learning.[61]

Goodman's "reformation" thinking regarding education is put succinctly.

1. Incidental education, taking part in the on-going activities of society, must again be made the chief means of learning and teaching.

2. Most high schools should be eliminated, with other kinds of youth communities taking over their sociable function.

3. College training should generally follow, rather than precede, entry into the professions.

4. The chief occupation of educators should be to see to it that the activities of society provide incidental education, rather than exploitation or neglect. If necessary, we must invent new useful activities that offer educational opportunities.

5. The purpose of elementary pedagogy, through age twelve, should be to relay socialization, to protect children's free growth, since our families and community both pressure them too much and do not attend to them enough.[62]

Berg's[63] *Education and Jobs: The Great Training Robbery* was a report of a careful and, in many instances, numerical study. It did not bear as directly on criticism or crisis in schools as did many other studies. But it dealt with the employability aspect of the school-society relationship as no other had done. The gist of Berg's analysis of this relationship is appropriate to present concerns. Berg was, above all, concerned to point out that higher education should enrich people's lives and not masquerade as a means of getting a job. Like Faltermayer[64] he challenged the validity of the B.S. degree. People leave universities in increasing numbers, go to work, become influential, and insist in more and more instances that job holders have degrees. The B.S. degree generates its own demand. (The same cycle affects the high school diploma.)

Berg is to be admired for rigorous comparisons of the educational attainments of job holders. Some of his conclusions were: (a) that the United States produces more B.S. degree holders than it needs; (b) that even if employers' specifications regarding education are accepted, educational attainment in the population surpassed job requirements in 1968; (c) that available evidence suggests that excess credentialism results in lower morale, higher turnover, and lower productivity; (d) that what is learned in college has little relationship to success and promotion; (e) that education and income are not nearly as highly correlated as many researchers suppose; (f) that worker dissatisfaction increases as educational levels increase for lower skilled jobs as well as for upper and middle level jobs; (g) that quality of ghetto education is not necessarily improved by teachers with better paper credentials; and (h) that paying teachers according to credits toward degrees encourages movement to other jobs in education and industry and deters upgrading of teachers. Berg would reverse the long-term tendency of employers to raise job entry requirements, challenge the credentials monopoly which schools enjoy and reform schools to find a balance between too much for some and not enough for others.

## Summary

Based on perceptions advanced in the mid 1960s through the early 1970s, one could conclude that schools were doomed beyond salvage. The more judicious conclusion is that it was fortunate that critics came to challenge the educational system at its very base. In *Who Needs Schools?*, Fischer pointed out that if all of the children of all of the people are to be educated, the idea that there need not be schools is an idle one. The question, Fischer said, is how to assure that schools do not ". . . reject psychologically and physically, vast numbers of children whose potentiality is neither determined nor developed".[65]

Career education was in every conceivable sense, a new response to (a) contemporary concern for individual students and equality of educational and other life opportunities, (b) contemporary conceptions of knowledge, storage and retrieval systems, and the value of practical and applied academic pursuits, (c) evidenced concern for young, black, female, and other "target groups," and (d) complaints about the nonconnectedness of school and society. Critics cry out for a more natural and easy transition from childhood to adulthood. Education is caught in the middle. In-school and out-of-school youth and adults of many ilks cry out with increasing frequency and volume for structured but meaningful and humanizing experiences which will help rather than hinder individual growth and development in a world where technology and jobs and forms of play change, but where what is human and humanizing changes little. As later chapters will show, many educational leaders and other influential people propose that career education is a proper bridge between youth and adulthood, education and work, school and community.

## A Postscript

This chapter was written to illustrate the climate in education preceding the emergence in 1971 of career education as a major national education priority. It was not intended that the chapter be a comprehensive treatment of past and present concerns for educational reform. However, it seems important to note that as this book goes to press the United States is engaged in the most widespread debate about education since the Sputnik era of the late 1950s. The catalyst for this debate was the publication in April 1983 of the report of the National Commission on Excellence in Education entitled *A Nation at Risk: The Imperative for Educational Reform.*[66]

In addition to the above study, several other books and reports were also published in 1983[67]. The general focus of these publications is concern about educational "quality" and "standards". The reader is urged to become familiar with these publications and to compare their perceptions with those discussed in this chapter. Individuals concerned about career education should become active in the debate about what education is and should be. People imbued with a career education philosophy can accept a majority of the conclusions and recommendations currently being offered, I believe. We should not be reluctant to embrace the idea that our "Nation is at risk" and that educational reform is imperative. (We should remind people that career education emerged in 1971 because of similar concerns about reform.)

On the other hand, we should respectfully challenge those recommendations with which we disagree. For example, the National Commission on Excellence in Education proposes what it calls "Five New Basics" for a high school curriculum consisting of four years of English; three years of mathematics, science, and social studies; and one-half year of computer science. Rather than simply accept this description of what is considered to be "basic", we should present the case that career education is also a basic and fundamental goal of education and that learning about and preparing for work is a prerequisite to a personally satisfying and socially productive adult life. We should have reform in education, but it should not be of the type that results in the schools focusing solely on the study of conventional, academic subject matter at the expense of all other important goals.

## REFERENCES

1.  Marland, S.P., Jr. Career Education Now. Address given at the Convention of the National Association of Secondary School Principals. Houston, Texas. January 23, 1971.

2.  Other important foundations of career education including the reorientation of vocational education, the career guidance movement, and theories and principles of career development are omitted from this chapter. Refer to the bibliography at the end of Chapter Two for related references.

3.  Postman, N. and Weingartner, C. *The School Book: For People Who Want To Know What All The Hollering Is About.* New York: Delacorte Press, 1973.

4.  McNally, H.J. and Passow, A.H. *Improving the Quality of Public School Programs.* New York: Teachers College Press, 1960.

5.  Leonard, G.B. *Education and Ecstasy.* New York: Dell Publishing, 1968.

6.  Ibid, p. 20.

7.  Ibid, p. 115.

8.  Ibid, p. 115.

9.  Ibid, pp. 215 & 216.

10. Conant, J.B. *The American High School Today.* New York: McGraw-Hill, 1959.

11. Postman, N. and Weingartner, C. *Teaching As A Subversive Activity.* New York: Dell Publishing, 1969.

12. Ibid, p. 151.

13. Dawson, H. *On the Outskirts of Hope.* New York: McGraw-Hill, 1968.

14. Clark, K. Alternative Public School Systems. In B. Gross and R. Gross (Eds.) *Radical School Reform.* New York: Simon and Schuster, 1969.

15. Ibid, pp. 120-121.

16. Glasser, W. *Schools Without Failure.* New York: Harper & Row, 1969.

17. Ibid, p. 199.

18. Brown, G. I. *Human Teaching for Human Learning: An Introduction to Confluent Education.* New York: Viking Press, 1971.

19. Purpel, D.E. and Belanger, M. (Eds.) *Curriculum and the Cultural Revolution.* Berkeley, California: McCutchan Publishing, 1972.

20. Barth, R.S. *Open Education and the American School.* New York: Agathon Press, 1972.

21. Purpel and Belanger, 1972, p. 486.

22. Martin, J.R. The Disciplinaries and the Curriculum. In D.E. Purpel and M. Belanger (Eds.) *Curriculum and the Cultural Revolution.* Berkeley, California: McCutchan Publishing, 1972, pp. 100-123.

23. Ibid, p. 102.

24. Ibid, P. 121.

25. Lamm, Z. The Status of Knowledge in the Radical Concept of Education. In D.E. Purpel and M. Belanger (Eds.) *Curriculum and the Cultural Revolution.* Berkeley, California: McCutchan Publishing, 1972, pp. 124-142.

26. Ibid, p. 127.

27. Ibid, pp. 128-129.

28. Gattegno, C. *What We Owe Children: The Subordination of Teaching to Learning.* New York: Outerbridge and Dienstfrey, 1970.

29. Purpel and Belanger, 1972, p. 485.

30. Featherstone, J. *Schools Where Children Learn.* New York: Liveright, 1971.

31. Kohl, H.R. *The Open Classroom: A Practical Guide to a New Way of Teaching.* New York: Random House, 1970.

32. Silberman, C.E. *Crisis in the Classroom: The Remaking of American Education.* New York: Random House, 1970.

33. Ibid, p. 203.

34. Ibid, pp. 207-208.

35. Schrag, P. End of the Impossible Dream. *Saturday Review,* 1970, 53(12), 60-61.

36. Ibid, p. 68.

37. Ibid, P. 92.

38. Ibid, P. 92.

39. See for example Burns, R.W. and Brooks, G.D. (Eds.). *Curriculum Design in a Changing Society.* Englewood Cliffs, New Jersey: Educational Technology, 1970.

40. Kerensky, V.M. and Melby, E.O. *Education II: The Social Imperative.* Midland, Michigan: Pendell Publishing, 1971.

41. Ibid, pp. 27-28.

42. Ibid, p. 67.

43. Ibid, pp. 99-100.

44. Illich, I. *Deschooling Society.* New York: Harper & Row, 1970 (a)

45. Illich, I. The False Ideology of Schooling. *Saturday Review,* 1970, 53(42), 56+ − 58+. (b)

46. Illich, I. The Alternative to Schooling. *Saturday Review,* 1971, 54(25), 44-48+.

47. Illich, 1970b, p. 58.

48. Illich, 1970a.

49. Illich, 1970a, p. 14.

50. Illich, 1971.

51. Illich, 1970a, pp. 78-79.

52. See for example Fischer, J.H. Public Education Reconsidered. *Today's Education,* 1972, 61(5), 22-31.

53. Berg, I. *Education and Jobs: The Great Training Robbery.* New York: Praeger Publishers, 1970.

54. Goodman, P. *New Reformation: Notes of a Neolithic Conservative.* New York: Random House, 1970.

55. Goodman, P. Visions: The School in Society. In B. Gross and R. Gross (Eds.) *Radical School Reform.* New York: Simon and Schuster, 1969, pp. 98-115.

56. Goodman, 1970, p. 67.

57. Goodman, 1969, p. 98.

58. Goodman, 1969, p. 103.

59. Goodman, 1970, p. 78.

60. Goodman, 1970, p. 81.

61. Goodman, 1970, p. 83.

62. Goodman, 1970, pp. 85-86.

63. Berg, 1970.

64. Faltermayer, E. Let's Break the Go-To-College Lockstep. *Fortune,* 1970, 82(5), 98-103+.

65. Fischer, J. H. Who Needs Schools? *Saturday Review,* 1970, 53(38), 78-79+.

66. *A Nation At Risk: The Imperative for Education Reform.* Report of the National Commission on Excellence in Education, Washington, D.C.: U.S. Government Printing Office, 1983.

67. *Action for Excellence.* Report of the Task Force on Education for Economic Growth, Denver, Colorado: Education Commission of the States, 1983. *Making the Grade.* Report of the Twentieth Century Fund Task Force on Federal Elementary and Secondary Education Policy, New York: The Twentieth Century Fund, 1983. Goodlad, J.A. *A Study of Schooling,* New York: McGraw-Hill, 1983. Boyer, E.L. *High School: A Report on Secondary Education in America,* New York: Harper and Row, 1983.

2

## THE CAREER EDUCATION MOVEMENT

---

### Introduction

The historical antecedents to career education extend back many years. However, the formal movement itself is generally acknowledged to have begun only in the early 1970s.

Without question or qualification, the person most singularly responsible for spurring career education was Sidney P. Marland, Jr. To be fully accurate, however, a history of career education must give credit to former Commissioner of Education James E. Allen, Jr., for his role in advancing the case for career education. In a 1970 speech before the National Association of Secondary School Principals, Allen appeared to have coined the term "career education":

> It is a renewed awareness of the universality of the basic human and social need for competence that is generating not only increased emphasis today on *career education*\* but a whole new concept of its character and its place in the total educational enterprise.[1]

A year later, Allen's successor as Commissioner, Sidney P. Marland, Jr., in a speech to the same group which Allen had addressed, launched an "idea" that grew into a national reform movement. Major sections from Marland's "Career Education Now"[2] speech are quoted below in recognition of the significance of his remarks.

> Uncertainty is the hallmark of our era. And because many educators have been unsure as to how they could best discharge their dual responsibility to meet the student's needs on the one hand and to satisfy the country's infinite social and economic appetites on the other, they have often succumbed to the temptation to point a God-like finger at vocational educators and damn them for their failure to meet the nation's manpower requirements and doubly damn them for their failure to meet the youngster's career requirements, not to mention his personal fulfillment as a human being.

---
\* emphasis added          22

Most of you are secondary school administrators. You, like me, have been preoccupied most of the time with college entrance expectations. Vocational-technical education has been a second-level concern. The vocational education teachers and administrators have been either scorned or condemned and we have been silent.

There is illogic here as well as a massive injustice. How can we blame vocational educators for the hundreds of thousands of pitifully incapable boys and girls who leave our high schools each year when the truth is that the vast majority of these youngsters have never seen the inside of a vocational classroom? They are the unfortunate inmates, in most instances, of a curriculum that is neither fish nor fowl, neither truly vocational nor truly academic. We call it general education. I suggest we get rid of it.

Whatever interest we represent, federal, state, or local, whether we teach or administer, we must perforce deny ourselves the sweet solace of knowing the other fellow is in the wrong. We share the guilt for the generalized failure of our public system of education to equip our people to get and hold decent jobs. And the remedy likewise depends upon all of us. As Dr. Grant Venn said in his book, *Man, Education, and Manpower:* "If we want an educational system designed to serve each individual and to develop his creative potential in a self-directing way, then we have work to do and attitudes to change."

The first attitude that we should change, I suggest, is our own. We must purge ourselves of academic snobbery. For education's most serious failing is its self-induced, voluntary fragmentation, the strong tendency of education's several parts to separate from one another, to divide the entire enterprise against itself. The most grievous example of these intramural class distinctions is, of course, the false dichotomy between things academic and things vocational. As a first step, I suggest we dispose of the term vocational education, and adopt the term career education. Every young person in school belongs in that category at some point, whether engaged in preparing to be a surgeon, a bricklayer, a mother, or a secretary.

How absurd to suggest that general knowledge for its own sake is somehow superior to *useful* knowledge. "Pedants sneer at an education that is useful," Alfred North Whitehead observed. "But if education is not useful," he went on to ask, "What is it?" The answer, of course, is that it is nothing. All education is career education, or should be. And all our efforts as educators must be bent on preparing students either to become properly, usefully employed immediately upon graduation from high school or to go on to further formal education. Anything else is dangerous nonsense. I propose that a universal goal of American education, starting now, be this: that every young person completing our school program at grade 12 be ready to enter higher education or to enter useful and rewarding employment.

Contrary to all logic and all expediency, we continue to treat vocational training as education's poor cousin. We are thereby perpetuating the social quarantine it has been in since the days of the ancient Greeks, and, for all I know, before then. Since the original vocational fields were defined shortly before World War I as agriculture, industry, and homemaking, we have too often taught those skills grudgingly — dull courses in dull buildings for the benefit of what we all *knew* were young people somehow prejudged not fit for college as though college were something better for everyone. What a pity and how foolish, particularly for a country as dependent upon her machines and her technology as America. The ancient Greeks could afford such snobbery at a time when a very short course would suffice to instruct a man how to imitate a beast of burden. We Americans might even have been able to afford it a half-century ago when a boy might observe the full range of his occupational expectations by walking beside his father at the time of plowing, by watching the farmers, blacksmiths, and tradesmen who did business in his home town.

But how different things are today and how grave our need to reshape our system of education to meet the career demands of the astonishingly complex technological society we live in. When we talk of today's career development, we are not talking about blacksmithing. We are talking about the capacity of our people to sustain and accelerate the pace of progress in this country in every respect during a lifetime of learning. And nothing less.

The question seems to be fairly simple, if we have the courage and creativity to face it: Shall we persevere in the traditional practices that are obviously *not* properly equipping fully half or more of our young people or shall we immediately undertake the reformation of our entire secondary education in order to position it properly for maximum contribution to our individual and national life?

I think our choice is apparent. Certainly continued indecision and preservation of the status quo can only result in additional millions of young men and women leaving our high schools, with or without benefit of diploma, unfitted for employment, unable or unwilling to go on to college, and carrying away little more than an enduring distaste for education in any form, unskilled and unschooled. Indeed, if we are to ponder thoughtfully the growing charge of "irrelevance" in our schools and colleges, let us look sharply at the abomination known as general education.

Of those students currently in high school, only three out of 10 will go on to academic college-level work. One-third of those will drop out before getting a baccalaureate degree. That means that eight out of 10 present high school students should be getting occupational training of some sort. But only about two of those eight students are, in fact, getting such training. Consequently, half our high school students, a total of approximately 1,500,000 a year, are being offered what amounts to irrelevant, general educational pap!

In pained puzzlement they toil at watered-down general algebra, they struggle to recollect the difference between adjectives and adverbs, and they juggle in their minds the atomic weight of potassium in non-college science. The liberal arts and sciences of our traditional college-preparatory curriculum are indeed desirable for those who want them and can use them. But there must be desire and receptivity, and for millions of our children, we must concede, such knowledge is neither useful nor joyful. They do not love it for its own sake and they cannot sell it in the career market place. Small wonder so many drop out, not because they have failed, but because we have failed them. Who would not at the earliest convenient and legal moment leave an environment that is neither satisfying, entertaining, or productive? We properly deplore the large numbers of young men and women who leave high school before graduation. But, in simple truth, for most of them dropping out is the most sensible elective they can choose. At least they can substitute the excitement of the street corner for the more obscure charms of general mathematics.

I want to state my clear conviction that a properly effective career education requires a new educational unity. It requires a breaking down of the barriers that divide our education system into parochial enclaves. Our answer is that we must blend our curricula and our students into a single strong, secondary system. Let the academic preparation be balanced with the vocational or career program. Let one student take strength from another. And, for the future hope of education, let us end the divisive, snobbish, destructive distinctions in learning that do no service to the cause of knowledge, and do no honor to the name of American enterprise.

It is terribly important to teach a youngster the skills he needs to live, whether we call them academic or vocational, whether he intends to make his living with a wrench, or a slide rule, or folio editions of Shakespeare. But it is critically important to equip that youngster to live his life as a fulfilled human being. As Secretary Richardson said, "I remind you that this department of government more than anything else is concerned with humaneness."

Ted Bell, now Deputy Commissioner for School Systems in OE, made the point particularly well in a recent speech to a student government group. He was speculating on the steps a young person needs to take not just to get a diploma or a degree today, but to make reasonably sure he will continue to learn in the years ahead, to be an educated man or woman in terms of the future, a personal future.

"Here," Dr. Bell said, "the lesson is for each person to develop a personal plan for lifelong learning: learning about the world we live in, the people that inhabit it, the environment — physical and social — that we find around us; learning about the sciences, the arts, the literature we have inherited and are creating; but most of all, learning the way the world's peoples are interacting with one another. If one educates himself in these things, he will have a pretty good chance of survival and a good life."

In other words, life and how to live it is the primary vocation of all of us. And the ultimate test of our education process, on any level, is how close it comes to preparing our people to be alive and active with their hearts, and their minds, and, for many, their hands as well.

True and complete reform of the high school, viewed as a major element of overall preparation for life, cannot be achieved until general education is completely done away with in favor of contemporary career development in a comprehensive secondary education environment. This is our ultimate goal and we realize that so sweeping a change cannot be accomplished overnight, involving as it does approximately 30 million students and billions of dollars in public funds.

Careful reading of the speech makes obvious how Marland's remarks relate to criticisms of education discussed in Chapter One. He spoke about "freeing the individual's precious potential," about concern for "humaneness," about "true and complete reform," and about how "Career education requires a new educational unity."

Without wishing to be critical of Marland, the preliminary nature of his proposals should also be noted. Marland did not define career education, but rather referred to a "concept" of career education. Lack of specificity was apparent also in his reference to *career education* and *vocational education* as seemingly synonymous terms, which resulted in a confusion of terms on the part of those who regarded career education as a new name for vocational education. Another statement that prompted considerable skepticism was Marland's comment that "all education is career education, or should be." Lastly, he directed most of his attention to the secondary school level excluding elementary, post-secondary, higher, and adult education levels. We shall see in the next section, however, how more definitive concepts of career education evolved in the months and years following the Marland speech.

## The Conceptualization and Development Era: 1971-74

Reactions to the "Career Education Now" speech were generally positive and enthusiastic. Concerted efforts within the U.S. Office of Education and in various other education and non-education settings were quickly initiated toward achieving the goals that Marland introduced. Several broad categories of activities will now be discussed to illustrate how career education evolved during the period 1971-74.

### Clarifying and Communicating the Concept

Marland's commitment to elevate career education to the level of a national education priority did not end with his inaugural speech. During his approximately one-and-a-half years tenure as Commissioner, Marland articulated his position on career education in numerous speeches, articles and interviews. He continued to iterate the key concepts of reform, humaneness, educational unity, and purpose-fulness of learning.

In part because of questions and concerns prompted by limita-tions of the speech noted earlier, he augmented his philosophy of career education in several ways. He clarified the fact that career education and vocational education were not synonymous, but that the latter was only a part of the former. He began to emphasize that career education was for all learners of all ages. His earlier statement that "career education is all of education" was reinterpreted to mean that career education is aimed at improving educational outcomes by relating all teaching and learning to the concept of career develop-ment. He never intended to imply literally that all education should be singularly focused on preparation for work at the exclusion of other equally important educational goals. He did, however, continue to refuse to define career education, believing instead (and properly so) that the federal role in education was to provide leadership, and that state and local education agencies should define what career education means to them.

Commissioner Marland was not the only member of the execu-tive branch of the federal government speaking on behalf of career education. In his 1972 State of the Union address, President Richard Nixon noted that:

Career education is another area of major new emphasis, . . . our schools should be doing more to build self-reliance and self-sufficiency, to prepare students for a productive and fulfilling life.

Career education provides people of all ages with broader exposure to and better preparation for the world of work. It not only helps the young, but also provides adults with an opportunity to adapt their own skills to changing needs, changing technology, and their own changing interests. It would not prematurely force an individual into a specific area of work but would expand his ability to choose wisely from a wider range of options. Neither would it result in a slighting of academic preparation, which would remain a central part of the educational blend.[3]

About a month later, Vice President Agnew in a speech to the American Association of School Administrators Convention, reaf-firmed the Nixon's administration's support for career education:

I regard career education as the most exciting new idea proposed in education in many years.

Every human being needs a sense of purpose, a goal to strive toward, and the pleasure of accomplishment when that goal is reached. It is a need that is built into the human soul and psyche. Career education offers hope that every American will have the chance to fulfill this need . . .[4]

The degree of national exposure and level of support given to career education at the highest echelons of the federal government was significant in helping to promote subsequent development of career education.

## Developing the Concept

Encouraged by the favorable response to his career education initiative, Marland planned and set into motion a series of administrative actions designed to begin the development, testing, and diffusion of career education. High[5] characterized this effort as a dual strategy involving two roles for the federal government.

*Federal research and development.* The first arm of this strategy called for carefully planned, systematic, and controlled research and development. This approach began in 1971 within the Office of Education but was transferred the next year to the National Institute of Education. It was concerned with the development of four different approaches to career education. These four "models" were described in a 1972 USOE briefing paper as follows:

### School-Based Model I

Objectives —
    To insure that students exit school with:
- A sense of purpose and direction.
- Self identity and identification with society (and an idea of their relationship).
- Basic skills and knowledge.
- A comprehensive awareness of career options and the ability to enter employment and/or further education.

The School-Based Career Education model is based on the infusion of career development objectives into comprehensive K-14 educational programs. Specifically, the purpose of this redirection is to acquaint students more intimately with a wide variety of career opportunities through each of their school experiences. This infusion must insure that every student receives an education which integrates his academic skills, social development and career preparation so that after high school his options are open for entering the labor market in a productive career or pursuing the post-high school education of his choice. Further, it must provide students with a continuing awareness of educational choices for career planning, which permits them to become fulfilled, productive, and contributing citizens.

Extensive guidance and counseling activities will help the student develop self-awareness, self-confidence, and mature attitudes, and will match his interests and abilities against potential careers. Placement into an entry-level job or further education is one of the ultimate goals for every student in the School-Based Career Education project.

## Employer-Based Model II*

Objectives —
  To insure that students exit school with:
  • A sense of purpose and direction.
  • Self identity and identification with society (and an idea of their relationship).
  • Basic skills and knowledge.
  • Specific skills and knowledge to be on a career path.

The Employer-Based Career Education project seeks to serve teen-age students through an optional out-of-school program. Many, of course, are characterized as the "disaffected, alienated and unmotivated." Although this optional program does accommodate such students, it is intended to be a real option for consideration by all students.

The Employer-Based Career Education will have as its goal the presentation of a comprehensive set of personalized educational experiences to secondary school students who voluntarily choose to participate in this mode of education instead of the traditional classroom curriculum.

Specifically, Employer-Based Career Education is an attempt to define individual learning elements with the curriculum, either existing or ideal, and to locate actual work or adult activity situations, managed by employers, in which students can learn these specific elements. Materials presented will be composed of all elements in the school curriculum, both academic and vocational in addition to other life skills. A special focus in the Employer-Based Model is the attempt to allow each student to participate in the selection of his own pattern of work or activity situations from a variety of opportunities, so that his learning situations are most relevant to his own interests and needs.

Participation in an Employer-Based Career Education project will provide students not only with the academic skills which are the center of the curriculum, but with familiarity and intimate experience in a variety of work situations of their own selection. It will allow students to function in a real adult-centered world. High school educational requirements will still be met, assuring high school graduation and an appropriate range of options upon graduation.

The Employer-Based Career Education projects will be operated by consortia of businesses and other organizations, both public and private. Such consortia are being formed presently under the sponsorship of Research for Better Schools, Inc., Philadelphia; the Far West Laboratory for Educational Research and Development, Berkeley, California; the Northwest Regional Educational Laboratory, Portland, Oregon, and the Appalachia Educational Laboratory, Charleston, West Virginia. They are operating under contract with the Office of Education, and have prime responsibility to develop and pilot test Employer-Based Career Education projects.

---

* This model was later renamed Experience-Based Career Education (EBCE).

### Home/Community-Based Model III

Objectives —
- To increase the employability and career options of out-of-school adults.
- To develop transportable processes and products.
- To conduct R & D programs aimed at the fractional objectives related to employability and career options.

The Home/Community-Based program is a career-oriented approach to enhance the employability and career options of out-of-school adults. Through the use of mass media, referral centers, individual counseling, and articulated exploration of community resources, adults will be able to identify their aspirations as they match their capabilities, experience and motivation to move through an adaptive program. The adult population may be reached through mass media; those who are excited into action must be handled by the limited, but expandable, capacities of existing service networks. The need for a central screening and switching mechanism will be met by the establishment of a total systems management entity. This systems management entity will involve representatives of the target populations, service agencies which will accommodate the target population adjustment/education/training/placement needs, employers, and other national/regional/local organizations which will participate in guiding or operating the program.

The Program will seek to: —

Use Mass Media to:
- Attract the attention of home/community-based populations.
- Probe the career education interests of these populations, and generate feedback about their needs.
- Provide information about existing career education resources.
- Inculcate certain skills related to engaging in career education.

Bring together existing career education agencies to:
- Coordinate their efforts to reach home/community-based population.
- Tackle problems of accessing the target population.
- Identify and attempt to fill gaps in service.
- Respond effectively to the emerging career education interests.
- Establish a central vehicle (the Career Education Extension Service) to carry out network functions:
  Receive and interpret feedback from home/community-based population.
  Refer individuals to existing agencies.
  Identify problems of access, and aid in their solution.
  Identify services gaps and assist in meeting them.
  Gather and disseminate information about promising approaches to career education and about the effectiveness of existing approaches to it.
  Systematically integrate all of the above.

It is a central theme of the Model to orchestrate, through the Career Education Extension Service, the use of mass media and the existing career education resources in order to help them reach and respond to the career education needs of home/community-based populations.

### Rural/Residential-Based Model IV

Objectives —

- To provide rural families with employment capabilities suitable to the area.
- To provide leverage on the economic development of the area.
- To improve family living.

The Rural/Residential Career Education Model is a research and demonstration project which will test the hypothesis that entire disadvantaged rural families can experience lasting improvement in their economic and social conditions through an intensive program at a residential center. The center is designing programs and will provide services for the entire family: day care; kindergarten, elementary and secondary education; family-living assistance; medical and dental services; welfare services; counseling; and cultural and recreational opportunities for single and married students and their families.

In addition to the education and social services systems a research and evaluation system, a management system, and a staff inservice training system is being designed and developed at the center. An economic development services plan for the local geographic region will also be designed. This plan will include a program of research on the educational services and programs required to improve the economic viability of the region and a program for expansion of regional efforts authorized under existing local, state and Federal programs in economic development. It is the intent of the project that students be able and ready to find employment in the local (6 state) region after completion of the program.[6]

*Assistance to state and local education agencies.* The second arm of the federal strategy for career education, as explained by High,[7] operated concurrently with the first. It consisted of providing financial support to state and local education agencies to encourage, stimulate and assist a wide variety of locally-developed innovations in career education. Funds for these activities were drawn from federal "discretionary" appropriations. That is, under various pieces of federal legislation, small percentages of the annual appropriations are reserved for use by the U.S. Commissioner of Education at his or her "discretion." Commissioner Marland chose to use discretionary funds available to him to support state and local pilot projects in career education.

The bulk of funds used to develop these early career education pilot programs came from vocational education appropriations. Part

C funds, totaling $18 million, were used to support two rounds of career education pilot projects. Each round was 18 months in duration and consisted of 56 grant awards, one in each state and territory. Part D funds, totaling approximately $47 million, were also used to support two rounds of projects. Each round was 36 months in duration, with 66 projects in the first round and 58 projects in the second round. Thus, during the first half of the 1970s a total of 236 career education projects were supported with a total of $65 million from Part C and Part D of the 1968 *Vocational Education Amendments* (P.L. 90-576). In actual practice, the total number of projects was several times larger than 236 since most state departments of education used their funds to "sub-contract" with various local schools, universities, or other public institutions. An index to these Part C and Part D project reports was compiled in a 1978 publication by Jezierski.[8]

## Embracing the Concept

Even though Marland's "Career Education Now" speech caught many people inside and outside of education off-guard (primarily because it was his first major speech as Commissioner of Education), it was not long until career education was being widely discussed and written about. Support for career education came quickly from many quarters. The sections that follow summarize activities, and provide evidence, of the magnitude of support for career education.

*The state of the States.* One measure of the degree of early support for career education was the extent to which various states engaged in activities supportive of career education. A November 1974 publication from the Office of Career Education[9] summarized the following: (a) Thirty states had approved definitions of career education and many other states had unofficial operational definitions. In some cases, a state's definition was written into law, while in others it was contained in a position paper or resolution. (b) Five states had enacted legislation specifically for career education. These mandates varied from those requiring broad implementation activities to those which were primarily directed at planning for future activities. (c) Twenty-five state legislatures had appropriated funds specifically earmarked for career education. Many other states had committed funds under existing budget categories. (d) Forty-two states and territories had designated Career Education Coordinators, and many states had funded additional staff especially to work in the area of career education.

*Endorsements by associations.* An interesting aspect related to the acceptance and growth of career education has been its appeal to a broad spectrum of individuals and groups representing diverse social, political, and educational philosophies. For example, career education was endorsed by a republican president in the 1972 State of the Union address and by the 1972 national plank of the Democratic Party. It has been supported by many of the giants of American business, industry and labor as well as some of the smallest community-based organizations. Humanists have advocated it because of its potential for contributing to the development of a more self-actualized person, and behaviorists have regarded it as a means to facilitate career development more systematically. It has been seen as having relevance for elementary and secondary education, higher education, adult and continuing education and for persons in their retirement years.

While career education obviously cannot be all things to all people, it nonetheless is general in its appeal of helping " . . . all individuals become familiar with the values of a work-oriented society, to integrate such values into their personal value systems, and to implement those values in their lives in such a way that work becomes possible, meaningful, and satisfying to each individual."[10] This excerpt is drawn from a 1975 publication by the Chamber of Commerce of the United States. The purpose of the publication was to express support for career education and to encourage leaders in education and leaders of business, industry, labor, professional, and community groups to work with each other on behalf of career education. The booklet reviewed briefly: (a) the nature of the career education concept, (b) why it was needed, (c) examples of success programs and practices, and (d) suggestions for group collaboration in career education. The booklet entitled *Career Education: What It Is and Why We Need It From Leaders of Industry, Education, Labor and the Professions* was developed in cooperation with the following groups.

The American Association of School Administrators – National Academy for School Executives

American Personnel and Guidance Association (now Association for Counseling and Development)

American Vocational Association, Inc.

Association of Community College Trustees

Bricklayers, Masons & Plasterers International Union of America

Council of Chief State School Officers

Distributive Education Clubs of America

General Federation of Women's Clubs

National Alliance of Business

National Association for the Advancement of Colored People
National Association of Elementary School Principals
National Association for Industry-Education Cooperation
National Association of Manufacturers
National Association of Secondary School Principals
National Congress of Parents and Teachers
National Federation of Business and Professional Women's Clubs
National Institute of Education
National Manpower Institute
National Organization for Women
National School Boards Association
National Urban League
Office of Education, Department of Health, Education, and
    Welfare
Vocational Industrial Clubs of America

*Local education agency, community college, and university efforts.* Earlier in this chapter it was discussed how federal monies were channeled to the states for research and development and for establishing career education pilot programs. These funded activities, however, represented only a portion of the total number of activities conducted. In *Career Education: The State of the Scene,* a 34 page chapter was devoted to describing innovations in career education, K-12. It was noted that:

> Available information indicates that career education is now taking place in approximately five thousand of our nation's seventeen thousand school districts. This growth is testimony to the attractiveness and substance of career education. Many of these five thousand school districts have excellent career education programs, developed over a period of three or four years. An even greater number of these programs are still in the formative stages. But wherever the program and whatever stage it is in, career education appears to have ignited the innovativeness of teachers, parents, administrators, counselors, and members of the business, labor, industry, and professional community.[11]

While career education was primarily implemented first in programs at the kindergarten through twelfth grade levels, an additional number of programs began to emerge at the college and university level (including two-year colleges) and for adults. Though some of these programs were not labeled as "career education," they were very compatible with the conceptual and programmatic aspects of career education. Chapter Five of the same publication cited above described nearly 30 of such programs.[12] They were grouped into six areas for discussion purposes. The areas were:

1.  Programs primarily engaged in providing consultant services in career education to local school systems and/or in providing inservice or preservice training in career education for teacher and other educational personnel;

2.  Programs within colleges or universities that have a broad interdepartmental base and provide a variety of approaches, including work experience, career counseling and guidance, flexible programming, and the like;

3.  Programs that contain "career counseling" as a major component either on college campuses or in other types of institutions;

4.  Programs that aim at serving specific target groups like business executives, senior citizens, full-time volunteers, "weekend" students, etc.;

5.  Programs that would be considered "noninstitutional" and which generally are based outside of colleges and universities. These are sometimes called "open schools" or "universities without walls"; and

6.  Programs that are institution-based but primarily focus on serving a constituency or student body that is normally not served by the instituion.

Clearly, career education beyond K-12 level was much more diverse than that for younger students. Equally clear is the fact that the type of innovations spurred at the post-secondary levels and beyond was prompted by the same desires for reform that launched the K-12 career education movement.

*Information dissemination.* By the end of 1971 it had become obvious that a major reform movement was underway, indicated in part by the explosion in the number and type of career education information products that began to emerge. "Career Education" first appeared as a descriptor in the subject index of *Research in Education* (RIE) in October 1971 and in the *Current Index to Journals in Education* (CIJE) in February 1972. (By 1984 the number of publications in RIE had grown to 6,140 and in CIJE to 2,177.)[13] During 1972 and 1973 over a dozen professional education journals devoted special issues to career education including such widely diverse journals as the *American Vocational Journal* (1972, 47(3)), *The Journal of Aesthetic Education* (1973, 4(4)), *Media and Methods* (1973, 9 (4)) and *Teaching Exceptional Children* (1973, 39(8)). Popular magazines also featured favorable articles about career education, for example, *Better Homes and Gardens* (October 1974) and *Changing Times* (April 1974).

In February 1972, the U.S. Government Printing Office published a monograph entitled *Career Education: A Handbook for Implementation*[14] that was a forerunner of many later career education textbooks. Much of the data in this early resource was subsequently incorporated into a commercial text entitled *Career Education: What It Is And How To Do It.*[15] (Refer to the end of this chapter for a list-

36                     Career Education for Teachers and Counselors

ing of the major textbooks on career education written between
1971 and 1983.)

A 1974 bibliography by Bailey[16] was one of the more comprehensive efforts to document the early literature on career education.
An interesting feature of his 267 page compilation was a listing of 19
biblographies on career education. In fact, one of the 19 was entitled
"A Bibliography of Bibliographies on Career and Vocational Education"!

The need for a timely, factual source of information about
career education for both policymakers and practitioners was satis-
fied when a career education subscription news service was initiated
in May 1972. Entitled *Career Education News,* this little newsletter
soon became required reading for all informed career educators and
itself had much to do with facilitating the further growth and development of the field. A second newsletter-type publication began in
1975 entitled *Education & Work.* In the fall of 1972 a group of Education Professions Development Act (EPDA) doctoral students at the
University of Missouri-Columbia initiated a quarterly *Journal of Career Education.* This journal continues today as a highly respected
source for scholarly and research articles in career education.*

Another early source of career education publications was the
Center for Vocational and Technical Education at The Ohio State
University. Among its early widely read career education documents
were *Review and Synthesis of Foundations for Career Education*[17]
and *Career Education Practice.*[18] The Center continued throughout
the 1970s to be a major publisher of Career Education resources and
instructional materials (recall that the Center was contractor for the
School-Based Model I). The National Center for Occupational Education at Raleigh, North Carolina was also active in career education
having published in 1973 a nine title *Career Education Monograph
Series.*[19]

In October 1973 the ERIC Clearinghouse in Career Education
was established at Northern Illinois University where it operated for
three years before being moved to The Ohio State University. The
Clearinghouse was responsible for accessing research and journal
articles into the national ERIC system and itself published a number
of career education information papers. These papers may be identified by referring to past indexes of *Research in Education* (now called
*Resources in Education*).

## Criticisms of Career Education

Career education is presented in this chapter in a predominantly
favorable light. Notwithstanding the author's obvious biases toward
career education, there have indeed been more positive aspects to

* In 1984, the title of the *Journal of Career Education* was changed to the *Journal
of Career Development.*

career education than negative ones. In the interests of objectivity, though, it must be acknowledged that career education has had its critics.

Some of the criticisms of career education are valid and reflect past and present shortcomings. Others are valid in the sense that different people have different philosophies about what education should be. That is, a philosophy of education which is intellectually honest may be valid even though it conflicts with career education. Certain criticisms, however, are invalid because they are based on inaccurate facts and/or perceptions of what career education actually is. All criticisms regardless of their origin deserve thoughtful study and debate by both advocates and critics. Following are discussions of the more frequently voiced criticisms made about career education during its early years.

*A new name for vocational education.* A number of people criticized career education for being a cosmetic title for vocational education. The basis for this confusion is easily explainable. First, even though Sidney Marland talked about a broad concept in his "Career Education Now" speech, he also seemed to equate career education with vocational education. For example: "I will indicate to you in a few moments . . . the steps we believe should be taken . . . to strengthen your hand in refashioning the vocational or career curriculum."[20] Second, as was pointed out earlier in this chapter, over $65 million dollars of vocational education funds were used to assist with the research and development of career education. It was only natural for people to assume that because vocational education monies were being spent, then the concept must really be vocational education. Finally, many of the early spokespersons and authors in career education like Rupert Evans, Louise Keller, Robert Taylor, Joel Magisos, Robert Worthington, Larry Bailey, and Ronald Stadt were vocational educators. (Refer to bibliography at end of chapter for titles of their publications.) Despite their leadership in career education, they tended to be seen by peers in terms of their vocational education identities.

*Vague and ill-defined; another fad from USOE.* Part of the strategy followed by Sidney Marland in promoting the development of career education was to decline to provide an explicit definition. This was based on his belief that the concept needed much national debate, much research, much scientific analysis, much testing of assumptions in real schools and classrooms before it could be given a dependable definition. Marland also believed that in order for the concept to succeed it must be perceived by teachers and school systems as something they choose to do rather than something proclaimed from Washington.[21]

Despite the seeming wisdom of this approach, some like Harold Howe (himself a former Commissioner of Education) argued that: "The concept is so general it runs the danger of being watered down into a mass of lip service activity that brings about no fundamental change in the schools."[22]

Closely related to those who criticized career education for being vague and ill-defined, were those critics who regarded the concept as just another fad perpetuated by the U.S. Office of Education. A 1973 article in *The American School Board Journal* provides a good example of this skepticism:

> . . . Remember *life adjustment* education? How about *family living* education? *Progressive* education? And that old, meaningless standby that still gets trotted out regularly: *quality* education?
>
> The junkyard of our educational heritage is strewn with decaying bandwagons that, in their time, generated enthusiasm in more or less direct proportion to their remedial ring. (Look-Say was supposed to make us a nation of readers; language laboratories were supposed to have us speaking French like Parisians.)
>
> Now comes a new Conestoga. Its wheels well greased with federal greenbacks, rolling westward from Washington with astonishing speed. Cheering chamber of commerce and overworked unemployment agencies already man the sideboards and, seemingly, the educational road ahead lies pockmarked with compelling reasons for school districts also to climb aboard.[23]

*Based on excessive claims and false assumptions.* While acknowledging that "there is much that is positive in the career education concept," Nash and Agne[24] voiced concern about the number of key assumptions left unexamined by career educators and about excessive claims and the absence of significant self-criticism. They observed that the career education literature accepts as an unchallenged good the continued existence of a corporate social order and a concept of human motivation that is achievement-motivated. A number of examples of career education programs and methods were cited to illustrate what they characterized as a "theory of learning based on four interrelated fallacies." They identified the fallacies as specialism, sequentialism, fundamentalism and credentialism. Nash and Agne dismissed the claim that career education is a means to educational reform by citing a Nixon speech on career education and then calling it "thinly guised politics."

Fitzgerald,[25] referring to career education as "an error whose time has come" maintained that the realities of labor markets and of jobs and job choices are such as to make career education a futile exercise. His arguments were that it is extremely difficult to make intelligent occupational decisions even if one wants to, that good jobs will probably not be available to all who want them, and that the satisfaction to be derived from work is over-rated. His pessimism is illustrated by his closing statement ". . . I would like all persons who want to work to be able to have a job, one which they feel is worth doing and which utilizes their true capabilities, yet leaves them the energy to enhance their lives and to participate in community with others. I can't quite believe that Career Education will make this a reality."[26]

*Is anti-intellectual and anti-humanistic.* Some of the better developed arguments against career education came from those who advocate traditional liberal education values. The Council for Basic Education published several statements that were cautious and hesitant toward career education.[27] While not taking its own unequivocal position on career education, the Council endorsed several critical statements by others who did.

Humanists were disquieted by the notion of career education and its potential effect on curriculum. They saw it as a rejection by the federal government of the liberal, humanistic tradition in education in favor of a strictly pragmatic, utilitarian approach focused entirely on employment and income. Career education was regarded as a euphemism for mechanistic job training.[28] Koerner sums up this type of criticism as follows:

> It is so uncompromisingly economic, so unabashedly narrow in conception, so relentlessly tied to the gross national product, and so anti-intellectual. What a commentary it would be on universal education if after a century and more of experience with public schooling. . . the nation were to accept the proposition that the greatest aim of its schools, their highest goal and ultimate purpose, was not to lead people toward a worthy and examined life, not to provide them with some grasp of the long cultural, esthetic and intellectual tradition of which they are a part – but that the highest goal is just to get people into jobs and to condition them to a life in the marketplace.[29]

*Is racially and sexually biased.* Minority criticisms of career education seemed to be based on false anticipation of what career education might become. Shirley Chisholm in a 1973 National Conference on Career Education Implications for Minorities speech " . . . expressed the opinion that Career Education is being designed for the children of the middle class and for working parents. She noted, for example, that one of the suggested activities for elementary students is to interview their parents about their careers. She questioned the relevance of such an assignment in a home where the father is unemployed, the mother is on welfare, the sister is a street walker, and the brother is a junkie."[30] Many of the concerns raised by black leaders, such as these, apparently grew out of a fear that career education represented a means to deny minorities full access to educational opportunity.

Female opposition toward career education grew out of reactions to a 1971 USOE film designed as part of a national dissemination effort to promote the concept.[31] Close scrutiny of the film by a number of women's groups revealed that scenes featuring men outnumbered those featuring women by about 90 to 50. Further, those scenes showing women usually depicted them in "traditional female jobs." Objections to the film resulted in its being withdrawn from use and later revised.

Some opposition by women was the result of more fundamental concerns. Edna Mitchell in a 1972 article[32] pointed out that career education had not recognized the seriousness of the "vocational miseducation" of girls. She pointed out that because "sex stereotyping begins in the crib," effective career education for girls would have to be "remedial" even in the elementary school.

*Leads to exploitation of young workers and displaces adult workers.* One of the central principles of career education is that youth should be provided with opportunities to try out various occupational roles in order to make more valid educational and occupational decisions. These experiences would have, as their primary purpose *learning* about occupations rather than *training* for occupations (i.e., the purpose of vocational education) and would be unpaid.

Organized labor, one of the more aggressive special interest groups in this country, regarded this practice as a threat to child labor laws, minimum wage laws, plant safety codes and displacement of adult workers. John Sessions, assistant director of the AFL-CIO's education department, reacted as follows to a 1973 career education planning document: "It is an atrocious document. I find nothing in the plan which treats unions as a constructive, creative resource in career education. References to unions invariably treat them as 'the enemy', a perverse obstacle to be overcome."[33] Sessions also criticized the *Employer-Based* career education model as "needlessly abrasive and not actually descriptive of what is going on." (The name of the model was changed in late 1973 to the *Experience-Based* model in large part due to criticism from organized labor).

The opposition to career education by organized labor is understandable in recognition of the fact that one of their roles is to advocate labor's historic social-political-educational-philosophies. More careful reading and consideration of their criticisms, however, suggests different motivations. Hoyt observed that: "One of the complaints of organized labor is that labor officials are not always members of policy advisory groups in career education. This is a valid complaint and one that we hope is now being overcome as communities plan for career education. Career education can't work without the support and involvement of labor."[34]

## A New Consensus

Two very significant events occurred in 1974 that helped to consolidate efforts of the previous three years as well as to provide new directions for the further development of career education. These two events are discussed below.

### USOE Policy Paper

In 1971 when Commissioner Marland established career education as a priority of the U.S. Office of Education, he emphasized the importance of *not* having an official USOE definition. As a result, by 1974 dozens of definitions had been proposed by various individuals and groups throughout the country.

In order to assess the degree of consensus regarding career education, a draft document was prepared by the Office of Education in February 1974. The draft document was submitted to a broad range of education leaders along with a study guide designed to elicit responses with respect to specific statements contained in the document. Analysis of the responses indicated a high degree of consensus for each of the 19 statements contained in the study guide. Following a number of minor revisions, the document entitled *An Introduction to Career Education: A Policy Paper of the U.S. Office of Education*[35] was officially adopted by the Office of Education in November 1974.

An important part of the paper was a listing of the following eleven conditions calling for educational reform. Note the similarity of these criticisms of American education with those summarized in Chapter One.

1.  Too many persons leaving our educational system are deficient in the basic academic skills required for adaptability in today's rapidly changing society.

2.  Too many students fail to see meaningful relationships between what they are being asked to learn in school and what they will do when they leave the educational system. This is true of both those who remain to graduate and those who drop out of the educational system.

3.  American education, as currently structured, best meets the educational needs of that minority of persons who will someday become college graduates. It fails to place equal emphasis on meeting the educational needs of that vast majority of students who will never be college graduates.

4.   American education has not kept pace with the rapidity of change in the postindustrial occupational society. As a result, when worker qualifications are compared with job requirements, we find overeducated and undereducated workers are present in large numbers. Both the boredom of the overeducated worker and the frustration of the undereducated worker have contributed to growing worker alienation in the total occupational society.

5.   Too many persons leave our educational system at both the secondary and collegiate levels unequipped with the vocational skills, the self-understanding and career decision-making skills, or the work attitudes that are essential for making a successful transition from school to work.

6.   The growing need for and presence of women in the work force has not been reflected adequately in either the educational or the career options typically pictured for girls enrolled in our educational system.

7.   The growing needs for continuing and recurrent education of adults are not being met adequately by our current systems of public education.

8.   Insufficient attention has been given to learning opportunities which exist outside the structure of formal education and are increasingly needed by both youth and adults in our society.

9.   The general public, including parents and the business-industry-labor community, has not been given an adequate role in formulation of educational policy.

10.  American education, as currently structured, does not adequately meet the needs of minority or economically disadvantaged persons in our society.

11.  Post high school education has given insufficient emphasis to educational programs at the sub-baccalaureate degree level.[36]

The purpose for citing criticisms of education was to introduce the case for career education as one of several possible responses to calls for educational reform. The concept of work was proposed as the vehicle for bringing about such reform. The notion of work was essential to the officially adopted USOE definition of career education as follows:

> *Career Education* is the totality of experience through which one learns about and prepares to engage in work as part of her or his way of living.[37]

In emphasizing preparation for work as the goal of career education, this definition provides a clearly recognizable reason for both educators and students to engage in education. It speaks both to the survival need of society for productivity and the personal need of all individuals to find meaning in their lives through their accomplishments. Work is a concept which reaches beyond economic survival to broader aspects of productivity in one's total life style.

## Separate Legislation

The majority of funds used to initiate and develop career education during the 1971 through 1974 period was provided through vocational education appropriations. Even though career education enjoyed enthusiastic support from the Nixon and Ford administrations and from the Congress, it was not until passage of Public Law 93-380 on August 21, 1974 that separate authorizations were provided. Section 406 (h) of the *Education Amendments of 1974* stated: "For purposes of carrying out the provisions of this section (406), the Commissioner is authorized to expend not to exceed $15,000,000 for each fiscal year ending prior to July 1, 1978."[38]

In addition to authorizing separate funding for career education, the 1974 Amendments contained the following five provisions:

*Office of Career Education.* In order to carry out the policies, purposes, and provisions of Section 406, an Office of Career Education was established in the U.S. Office of Education. The Office was headed by a Director who reported directly to the Commissioner.

*National Advisory Council.* A National Advisory Council was established consisting of twelve public members broadly representative of the fields of education, the arts, the humanities, the sciences, community services, business and industry, and the general public. The Council's role was to provide advice to the Commissioner of Education and to the Congress concerning implementation of the Act.

*Survey and Assessment.* The Advisory Council with the assistance of the Commissioner's office was charged with conducting a nationwide survey and assessment of the status of career education programs, projects, curricula, and instructional materials and to submit a report to the Congress. A summary of the study is provided later in this chapter.

*Demonstration Grants and Exemplary Models.* Most of the funds authorized under Section 406 were for grants to demonstrate the most effective methods and techniques in career education and to develop exemplary career education models. Grants were used to fund programs related to five different purposes.

(a)  Activities designed to effect incremental improvements in K-12 career education through one or a series of exemplary projects;

(b)  Activities designed to demonstrate the most effective methods and techniques in career education in such settings as the senior high school, the community college, or in institutions of higher education;

(c)   Activities designed to demonstrate the most effective methods and
      techniques in career education for such special segments of the pop-
      ulation as handicapped, minority, low income, or female youth;

(d)   Activities designed to demonstrate the most effective methods and
      techniques for the training and retraining of persons for conducting
      career education programs; and

(e)   Activities designed to communicate career education philosophy,
      methods, program activities, and evaluation results to career educa-
      tion practitioners and to the general public.

*Grants for State Planning.* Grants were also awarded to state
education agencies to encourage state-wide planning for career education and to foster articulation between state agencies and local
education agencies.

## National Survey and Assessment of the Status of Career Education

One of the mandates of Section 406 of the *Education Amendments of 1974* was that the Commissioner of Education, in cooperation with the National Advisory Council for Career Education, carry
out a survey and assessment to determine the present status of career
education programs and practices. Accordingly, a contract was awarded by the Office of Education to the American Institutes of Research
to conduct the study.[39]

The survey was performed between June 1975 and May 1976
and was based on data pertaining to the 1974-75 school year. Data
were collected from 806 respondents from a representative sample of
900 local school districts nationwide; from 50 state education agencies; and from 630 respondents of the 839 members of the American
Association of Colleges for Teacher Education. In addition, 797 commercial and 2,193 noncommercial instructional materials in career
education were cataloged.

The complete 322 page study contained a wealth of descriptive
data and findings. Among the more important conclusions were the
following:

> Of nine learner outcomes of career education proposed by USOE (1975),
> all were rated by local school districts as somewhere between "important"
> and "absolutely necessary." The implementation of activities to achieve
> these outcomes was gradual, however, with a majority of survey respon-
> dents describing their districts' efforts as "now limited." Although a majori-
> ty of the nation's school districts were engaged in at least some staff devel-
> opment activities in career education, only 3% had taken all five steps of
> obtaining funds, allocating staff, writing a formal policy, forming an
> Advisory Committee, and carrying out formal evaluations with respect to
> career education. Approximately 20% of the nation's teachers have been
> involved in career education activities. Of fifteen student career education

activities assessed, although half of the nation's students were in school districts in which at least one was implemented broadly, only a fifth were in districts that had implemented over half the activities broadly and only 3% were in districts where all had been implemented broadly. Funding needs were frequently mentioned as critical to the further development of career education in the local districts.

A clear dichotomy was apparent in the activities reported by the local districts "to help young people learn about and prepare to engage in work as a part of their way of living." There were activities that had been carried on traditionally as a part of educators' concerns that their students be prepared to cope with society when leaving school, and there were the innovative activities that were being introduced as a part of the current national career education movement. Although the distinction between the two types of activity is not altogether obvious in practice, the innovative activities were roughly identifiable as those tending to occur in districts in which formal career education policy statements had been or were being written. These activities differed from the traditional activities on two notable dimensions: they tended to be carried out in the earlier grades — traditional activities relating school to work were almost exclusively at the secondary level; and they tended to be carried out by teachers rather than counselors — counselors have long played a role that significantly overlaps the career educator role, so their involvement in these activities is not as novel as the involvement of classroom teachers.

Increased community involvement emerged as an essential component of successful career education programs: levels of activity were higher where representatives of the business, labor, and industrial community were reported involved. Also, the activities most frequently reported as effective in helping young people learn about and prepare for work all involved bringing students together with work world representatives in one way or another.

At the state level, there was a remarkable variation of activities to promote career education in different states. Although most state education agencies had policy statements on career education, very few states had enacted specific legislation supporting career education. In most local districts in which the level of career education activity was high, there was acknowledgment that the state education agency impact on a few local school districts, through demonstration projects, was much greater than on the majority of districts.

In the teacher training institutions, there was a great deal of discussion of career education; however, the implementation of actual career educator training programs was not yet at a significant level. Few schools of education allocated as much as 3% of their budgets to career education programs. The need, so strongly stated by local school districts and State education agencies, for help in developing the school staffs into career education, was only beginning to be met by the colleges for teacher education.

Throughout the country, the words "career education" were being heard ever more frequently, and the USOE guidelines were receiving much discussion and were having an impact in many localities. In the one-quarter of responding districts in which career education efforts were described as based on those guidelines, the level of career education activity was higher than in the other three-quarters of the districts. In terms of a pervasive reform of education, career education was beginning to have a visible impact on schools across the country in 1974-75. Its acceptance and implementation were still tentative, however, as many school districts waited to see whether "it really works."[40]

## 1976 Legislation

In October 1976, Congress passed the *Education Amendments of 1976* (P.L. 94-482). The primary purpose of the legislation was the reauthorization of programs and funding for (a) higher education, (b) vocational education, and (c) the National Institute of Education. The law also contained a Part C of Title III entitled "Career Education and Career Development." This legislation is of interest primarily from a historical standpoint.

According to High,[41] Part C was apparently inserted into the legislation by the Senate Committee on Human Resources. It is not clear what or who motivated them to do so. The House of Representatives never looked very favorably on Part C, because the House had already begun the formulation of legislation that was eventually to be enacted as the *Career Education Incentive Act*.

It should be noted that P.L. 94-482 only authorized Part C for Fiscal Year 1978. Obviously, this "one-shot" kind of program had little potential to produce any significant changes. In any event, Congress never appropriated any money to implement Part C, probably because: (a) There was an almost total lack of interest and/or support from either the Administration or the House of Representatives, and (b) Career educators did not feel any pressing need for Part C to be funded. It should be remembered that Congress had provided $10 million per year for career education from Fiscal Years 1975 through 1978 under the authority of Section 406 of P.L. 93-380. When that legislation expired, P.L. 95-207 picked up funding authority for Fiscal Years 1979 through 1983. Thus, Part C was not essential to the continuity of the Federal effort in career education.

### The Commissioner's National Conference on Career Education

As part of the celebration of the Bicentenary year of our nation, the U.S. Office of Education sponsored in 1976 a number of national education conferences. One conference, held in Houston, Texas on November 7-10, 1976 was devoted to career education. Hoyt attributed the idea for the conference to a group of local K-12 career education coordinators who participated in "Mini-Conference #14" sponsored by the Office of Career Education in July 1974. "These career education practitioners voiced a need to interact with their counterparts throughout the United States. They felt they had much to share and much to learn from such interaction. Their dream was to gather together all kinds of 'actors' in career education — teachers, counselors, administrators, business/industry personnel, representatives from organized labor, parents, students, and government — for purposes of improving the expertise of each."[42]

More than 8,200 people gathered at the Texas-sized Astrohall to participate in workshops, general sessions and frequent coffee breaks to exchange ideas and reaffirm their own commitment to the ideals of career education. The conference was officially launched the morning of November 8 with an address by Sidney P. Marland, Jr. Dr. Marland set the tone for the next two and half days with his enthusiastic and thoughtful comments. Following are excerpts from the address:

> I feel a great sense of joy — not to mention awe — in looking upon this assembly and contemplating the extraordinary power that is now gathered in this room. It is gathered around a single idea that has brought us together in common purpose. That idea is career education.
>
> It is not a new idea. It was not a new idea in 1971. It has been an underlying concept of civilized people's self-development since the beginning — that is, *growing up to work.* But somehow, over the generations education had come to mean schooling — and learning had come to mean something that happens only in schools and colleges — and that growing up to work was something that happened *outside* schools and colleges, and never the twain should meet.
>
> Career education's message was and remains, a sincere call for reform, that says the two are rightly inseparable — that work is not mean or repulsive, and that education has a very essential part to play, at all grades, and for all ages, in helping people ready themselves for work — intellectually, socially, economically, emotionally, yes, spiritually.
>
> The reform applies to the schools and colleges, but it also asks for reform in those other places that contribute so much to the education of our people *outside* classrooms. It asks for new commitments from business, labor and industry — from governments at Federal, state and local levels. It asks for a larger order of humanness from the American people altogether as they attempt to enlighten the lives of others, especially the young, through better education . . . not only that which happens in schools and colleges.
>
> One of the first goals of the career education philosophy is to make the idea of work understandable — even by the very young in our elementary schools. Work is *not*, as Oscar Wilde once said — the curse of the drinking class. Work is something that all of us do — whether for profit, for psychic fulfillment, for leisure fun, or through compassion and care for others. But work we do — or we are vegetables.

> All kinds of work are to be honored — from the honest and neces-
> sary ministrations of the cobbler and the window cleaner to the awesome
> skills of the computer analyst and the surgeon. Work, career education
> teaches, is good, necessary and joyful . . . and people — young people
> especially — ought to know much more about it in its thousands of differ-
> ent modes, and know much more about themselves, their aptitudes and
> their competencies for work.[43]

Marland went on to discuss the roles of business, labor, industry,
government, education and the general public in working together
on behalf of career education. He closed his speech on a reflective
note:

> There were many six years ago, who noted archly that career educa-
> tion was a passing fad — that like its many predecessor attempts to reform,
> it, too, would pass. This meeting today is ardent witness to their error. But
> if, over the next five to ten years, we do our work well, there will no longer
> be a need to speak of career education. We will speak again of education —
> for it will have changed.[44]

There has probably never been an education conference that
brought together a wider variety of individuals and groups all devoted
to a singular concept. Three main types of activities were conducted.
First, four General Sessions were held at which keynote speakers
addressed large audiences in the thousands. Second, there were eight
Theme Sessions consisting of panel discussions of a particular topic
like "Career Education: Who Needs It?" or "Career Education: What
Proof Do We Have That It Works?" Finally, there were six different
"clusters" of presentations as follows:

Cluster A — Career Education By Level and Settings (20)

Cluster B — Career Education, By Function (30)

Cluster C — Career Education, By Special Population Groups
(11)

Cluster D — Educational Skills and Approaches (44)

Cluster E — Career Education Community Resources (31)

Cluster F — Career Education Concepts (18)

The number in parentheses above indicates how many topics were
scheduled related to each cluster. These topics in turn consisted of
individual presentations averaging about five presenters each. A total
of nearly 1,000 speakers discussed almost every conceivable aspect of
career education theory and practice. A compilation of abstracts
summarizing each presentation was later published under the title of
*Career Education: A Collaborative Effort.*[45]

## The Career Education Incentive Act

The National Advisory Council for Career Education, first established by the *Education Amendments of 1974,* was sworn into office on March 31, 1975. Included among its duties was that of "... determining the need for further legislative remedy in order that all citizens may benefit from the purposes of career education ..." Toward that end, the council forwarded to Congress in November 1975 a report containing nine major recommendations for new career education legislation.

Less than a month after the council submitted its "Interim Report with Recommendations for Legislation",[46] Representative Perkins introduced a bill in the House of Representatives that was virtually identical to the Council's proposal. Even though this particular bill was not passed before Congress adjourned in 1976, a similar bill was passed the following year. It was entitled the *Career Education Incentive Act* (P.L. 95-207) and became law on December 13, 1977. A comprehensive account of the history of this legislation is contained in a 1979 doctoral dissertation by Charek.[47] The purpose of the legislation was contained in Section 3:

> In recognition of the prime importance of work in our society and in recognition of the role that the schools play in the lives of all Americans, it is the purpose of this Act to assist states and local educational agencies and institutions of postsecondary education, including collaborative arrangements with the appropriate agencies and organizations, in making education as preparation for work, and as a means of relating work values to other life roles and choices (such as family life), a major goal of all who teach and all who learn by increasing the emphasis they place on career awareness, exploration, decisionmaking, and planning, and to do so in a manner which will promote equal opportunity in making career choices through the elimination of bias and stereotyping in such activities, including bias and stereotyping on account of race, sex, age, economic status, or handicap.[48]

The three main features of the legislation were the: (a) authorization for a state plan/state allotment program of federal assistance for the implementation of elementary and secondary career eduction, (b) authorization for a discretionary grant program to support projects demonstrating career education at the postsecondary level, and (c) authorization for a small discretionary grant program to support model projects demonstrating career education at the elementary/secondary level. A total of $325 million was authorized for Fiscal Years 1979 through 1983. Of most interest to K-12 local education agency personnel was Section 8 (3) which identified how local schools might employ funds received under the act:

(A)  instilling career education concepts and approaches in the classroom;

(B)  developing and implementing comprehensive career guidance, counseling, placement, and followup services utilizing counselors, teachers, parents, and community resource personnel;

(C)  developing and implementing collaborative relationships with organizations representing the handicapped, minority groups, and women and with all other elements of the community, including the use of personnel from such organizations and the community as resource persons in schools and for student field trips into that community;

(D)  developing and implementing work experiences for students whose primary purpose is career exploration, if such work experiences are related to existing or potential career opportunities and do not displace other workers who perform such work;

(E)  employing coordinators of career education in local educational agencies or in combinations of such agencies (but not the individual school building level);

(F)  training of local career education coordinators;

(G)  providing inservice education for educational personnel, especially teachers, counselors, and school administrators, designed to help such personnel to understand career education, to acquire competencies in the field of career education and to acquaint such personnel with the changing work patterns of men and women, ways of overcoming sex stereotyping in career education, and ways of assisting women and men to broaden their career horizons;

(H)  conducting institutes for members of boards of local educational agencies, community leaders, and parents concerning the nature and goals of career education;

(I)  purchasing instructional materials and supplies for career education activities;

(J)  establishing and operating community career education councils;

(K)  establishing and operating career education resource centers serving both students and the general public;

(L)  adopting, reviewing, and revising local plans for coordinating the implementation of the comprehensive program; and

(M)  conducting needs assessments and evaluations.[49]

It is important to recognize that Congress neither asked nor demanded that career education be implemented. Congress' motivation can be inferred from the fact that the word "incentive" was used in the title. This legislation was not intended to be a continuing grant program. Rather, relatively small sums of money were authorized for a five year period to assist state and local school districts with "start up" costs.[50]

Aspirations of the Office of Career Education regarding what might be accomplished in the five-year time frame provided by this law were outlined by Hoyt.[51] These were intended to be general strategies illustrative of what needed to be accomplished toward fulfilling the intent of the Congress. They are repeated below in abbreviated form.

By the end of the 1978-79 school year, it is my hope that a general strategy will have been employed that sees the concept of career education (a) defined with community input (b) in terms consistent with the law (c) in ways that reflect obviously recognized community needs (d) that recognize the need for community participation in implementation and (e) represents a relatively low cost "people effort" rather than carrying any kind of "program add-on" implications.

By the end of the 1979-80 school year, it is my hope that: (a) a massive career education infusion effort will have taken place in the K-12 school system; (b) strategies for involving community youth organizations in the career education effort will have been devised and implemented; and (c) initial strategies for involving adult community groups in the career education effort will have been formulated and implemented.

By the end of the 1980-81 school year, it is my hope that a concerted nationwide attempt will have been made to implement a comprehensive career education effort with a high degree of cooperation existing between the education system and a key nucleus of community organizations. If comprehensive efforts can be assured, it is my further hope that high priority will be given to careful evaluations of career education's effectiveness.

By the end of the 1981-82 school year, I would hope that beginning collaborative career education efforts could be mounted in many communities. By this time, of course, federal funds can only pay up to 50 percent of the costs for implementing career education with the other 50 percent coming from state and/or local funds. If responsibility for the effectiveness of career education is to be shared between the education system and the broader community, so must its "ownership" be shared. The school system must be willing to give away part of the ownership and the broader community must be willing to accept it. It is unreasonable to expect that the process will be completed in many communities by the end of the 1981-82 school year, but it is essential that it originates.

By the end of the 1982-83 school year, it seems wise to me to adopt a general strategy that calls for federal funds to be used only in those communities where a true community collaborative career education effort is in place. By that time, 75 percent of the operating costs will be borne by states and/or local communities. The federal government will be out of the picture in terms of providing direct financial assistance by the end of the 1982-83 school year. That part of the intent of the Congress will have been met.

## Office of Career Education Leadership

One provision of Section 406 of the *Education Amendments of 1974* was the creation of an Office of Career Education within the U.S. Office of Education. The Office was to be headed by a Director who reported directly to the Commissioner of Education. Kenneth B. Hoyt, a Professor of Education at the University of Maryland and nationally known counselor educator was named the first Director.

Whereas Sidney Marland was the key figure in launching the career education movement, Kenneth Hoyt was the key figure in guiding it through its formative years. Displaying the enthusiasm, commitment and tireless energy more typical of an evangelist than a bureaucrat, Hoyt (assisted by able staff persons like Sidney High and John Lindia) made significant contributions in three areas: (a) achieving a *consensus* regarding the definition and purpose of career education, (b) *communicating* the theory and practice of career education, and (c) helping to develop a nationwide *constituency* supportive of career education.

An early concern of Hoyt's upon joining the Office of Education was the need to consolidate various concepts and definitions of career education into some type of consensus statement. It will be recalled that Sidney Marland did not define career education, believing instead that states, local education agencies, and individual scholars should achieve that for themselves. So successfully was this accomplished that by 1974 Hoyt felt the time had come to integrate these various ideas and concepts. He prepared a draft document entitled "An Introduction to Career Education" and submitted it to nearly 300 persons for review and comment. The outcome of this process was the subsequent publication of the career education policy paper discussed earlier in this chapter. The definition contained in the policy paper has since become the most widely quoted and accepted definition of career education.

Another significant accomplishment by Hoyt was the improvement of communications about career education and the development of many different types of publications and resource documents. In order to assist local level practitioners a number of "how-to-do-it" resources were compiled and disseminated. An excellent *Bibliography on Career Education*[52] was published in May 1973 and again in July 1979. A series of short topical publications entitled *Monographs on Career Education* was initiated in which a number of recognized authorities were commissioned to address major theoretical concepts and issues. The National Advisory Council for Career Education (NACCE) working closely with Hoyt and his staff issued 24 publications designed to fill in major "knowledge gaps" in career education. A listing of *Monographs* and NACCE publications is provided at the end of this chapter.

Perhaps Hoyt's greatest success was in helping to build a national constituency supportive of career education. Employing his considerable political skills, low-key interpersonal style, and pragmatic philosophy, he cultivated working relationships with many different groups. Hoyt took to the lecture circuit accepting dozens of invitations to address local, regional and national meetings on a variety of career education topics. A collection of over 30 of his speeches was published in 1975 under the title of *Career Education: Contributions to an Evolving Concept.*[53] In addition to his hectic travel schedule, he brought people to Washington to meet with him. A "mini-conference" format was used to invite a small group of people representing a particular constituency (e.g., the National Alliance of Business, Women's American ORT). Participants in each mini-conference developed their own agenda by listing topics or issues they thought pertinent to discuss. The list of topics or issues provided the basis for an informal, extended discussion (usually two days) which Hoyt chaired and recorded notes. Summaries of most of these mini-conferences were published as separate titles in the *Monographs on Career Education* series.

In cultivating these various relationships (he prefers the term "collaboration"), Hoyt was astute to ally himself with classroom teachers. He continually referred to career education as a "grassroots" phenomenon. His monograph entitled *K-12 Classroom Teachers and Career Education: The Beautiful People* is a good example of this orientation.[54] Remember that the Commissioner's National Conference on Career Education discussed earlier in this chapter grew out of an idea and commitment emanating from one of these mini-conferences.

In March 1981, the organization of career education within the federal government changed. The U.S. Office of Career Education had been established by the Education Amendments of 1974 and reported directly to the Commissioner of Education. In 1980 after the new Department of Education was created, the career education office reported to the Office of Educational Support. In the latest reorganization, career education was changed from an "office" to a "division" under the Office of Educational Support. The change was apparently made to reflect more accurately the then current bureaucratic setup within the Department of Education.[55] One accomplishment of the new division was to produce a *Selected Bibliography on Career Education* published in April 1983.[56]

On August 1, 1982, Kenneth B. Hoyt left the Department of Education to return to academe. His departure, along with the previously discussed change in organization of the Office of Career Education, marked the end of an era. As the first and only Director of the U.S. Office of Career Education, Hoyt masterfully used the status and influence of his office to promote and extend career education. He will forever be remembered for his national leadership on behalf of career education.

## Education Consolidation

The election of Ronald Reagan as President in 1980 brought with it a new philosophy of government. This philosophy, called the "New Federalism," had as one of its goals that of reducing the size, cost, and complexity of government. To this end, the Reagan administration developed and the 97th Congress passed on August 13, 1981 the Omnibus Reconciliation Act. Title V of this Act was called the "Omnibus Education Reconciliation Act of 1981."[57]

Chapter Two of Title V is an amalgamation of many former catgorical programs. Its purpose was to combine about 30 small programs into one large block grant. Even though career education was one of the programs combined into Chapter Two, funding for career education remained separate in fiscal year 1982 because federal funds were made available that year under the Career Education Incentive Act. In fiscal year 1983, career education was placed in the block grant program.

Authorization for career education continues as one of several "special projects" eligible for Chapter Two funds. In theory, the education reconciliation act provides state and local education agencies with opportunities to exercise their own preferences and operating procedures. Hopefully, large numbers of states and localities will designate career education as a priority for support.

## Summary

Skeptics who in 1971 labeled career education a "fad", "glorified vocational education", or "another ill-conceived proposal from the U.S. Office of Education", must surely be having second thoughts. An article published in the December 1979 *Phi Delta Kappan* discussed the ten most significant events of the decade. Career education was identified as one of the ten. According to the author:

> The average life of an educational reform in the U.S. is about three years. Career education, introduced in 1971 with much fanfare, has outlived most efforts to reform some aspect of schooling. At the end of the decade career education was still alive and doing well, or doing something, in probably a fourth of the nation's school districts.

Despite its vagueness, Marland's idea generated enormous public interest, caught the fancy of Congress, and gave rise to a stream of speeches, articles, research studies and books . . .

Always a concept in search of a definition, career education was the decade's moderate success story. Countless teachers, for the first time, helped students discover their interests and aptitudes, provided them with facts about the world of work, and called it career education . . .[58]

This is not to suggest that major issues in career education have all been resolved. The successful implementation of career education *will continue to require* aggressive leadership; adequate sums of money; commitment to the reform of public schools, state education agencies, and teacher education programs; education of parents and lay citizens; and an infinite amount of perseverance and hard work. However, the acceptance of career education by a broad range of constituencies is encouraging evidence that a large number of people are willing to accept the challenge.

## REFERENCES

1. Allen, J.E., Jr. "Competence for All as the Goal for Secondary Education." Address given at the Convention of the National Association of Secondary School Principals. Washington, D.C., February 10, 1970.

2. Marland, S.P., Jr. "Career Education Now." Address given at the Convention of the National Association of Secondary School Principals. Houston, Texas. January 23, 1971.

3. Nixon, R.M. "Comments on Career Education." State of the Union Address, January 20, 1972.

4. Agnew, S.T. "Untitled Speech." Address given at the Convention of the American Association of School Administrators. Atlantic City, New Jersey, February 16, 1972.

5. High, S.C., Jr. "Career Education: A National Overview." *School Science and Mathematics Journal,* 1976, 76(4), 276-284.

6. *Education Briefing Paper.* Washington, D.C.: U.S. Office of Education, June 15, 1972.

7. High, S.C., Jr., 1976

8. Jezierski, K., Ed. *Index of Interim, Supplemental, and Final Reports from Career Education Pilot Projects Supported Under Part C and Part D of Public Law 90-576.* Columbus, Ohio: The National Center for Research in Vocational Education, May 1978.

9. *Career Education: The State of the Scene.* Washington, D.C.: Office of Career Education, November 1974.

10. *Career Education: What It Is and Why We Need It from Leaders of Industry, Education, Labor and the Professions.* Washington, D.C.: Chamber of Commerce of the United States of America, 1975, p. 4.

11.  *Career Education: The State of the Scene,* 1974, p. 123.

12.  Ibid, pp. 159-197.

13.  *Thesaurus of ERIC Descriptors.* Phoenix, Arizona: Oryx Press, 1984, p. 34.

14.  *Career Education: A Handbook for Implementation.* Washington, D.C.: U.S. Government Printing Office, February 1972.

15.  Hoyt, K.B., Evans, R.N., Mackin, E.F. and Mangun, G.L. *Career Education: What It Is and How to Do It.* Salt Lake City, Utah: Olympus Publishing Company, 1972.

16.  Bailey, L.J., Ed. *Facilitating Career Development: An Annotated Bibliography, II.* Carbondale, Illinois: Department of Occupational Education, Southern Illinois University, February 1974.

17.  Herr, E.L. *Review and Synthesis of Foundations for Career Education.* Columbus, Ohio: The Center for Vocational and Technical Education, March 1972.

18.  Budke, W.E., Bettis, G.E., and Beasley, G.F. *Career Education Practice.* Columbus, Ohio: The Center for Vocational and Technical Education, December 1972.

19.  Morgan, R.L. and Shook, M.W., Eds. *Career Education Monograph Series.* Raleigh, North Carolina: Center for Occupational Education, 1973.

20.  Marland, 1971, p. 1.

21.  Marland, S.P., Jr. *Career Education: A Proposal for Reform.* New York: McGraw-Hill Book Company, 1974, p. 84.

22.  "Career Education: For Some the New Idea; For Others the New Order." *The American School Board Journal,* 1973, 160 (6), p. 28.

23.  Ibid, p. 27.

24.  Nash, R.J. and Agne, R.M. "Career Education: Earning a Living or Living a Life?" *Phi Delta Kappan,* 1973, 54(6), 373-378.

25.  Fitzgerald, T.H. "Career Education: An Error Whose Time Has Come." *School Review,* 1973, 82 (1), 91-105.

26.  Ibid, p. 104.

27.  "Professional Dissent In Career Education." In E.L. Herr, *The Emerging History of Career Education: A Summary View.* Washington, D.C.: National Advisory Council for Career Education, 1976, pp. 283-290.

28.  Marland, S.P., Jr. "Meeting our Enemies: Career Education and the Humanities". *English Journal,* 1973, 62, 900-906.

29.  "Career Education: For Some the New Idea; for Others the New Order." 1973, p. 28.

30.  *Career Education: Current Trends in School Policies & Programs.* Arlington, Virginia: National School Public Relations Association, 1974, p. 24.

31.  Ibid, pp. 24-25.

32.  Mitchell, E. "What about Career Education for Girls?" In J. W. Fuller and T.D. Wheaton, *Career Education: A Lifelong Process,* Chicago, Illinois: Nelson-Hall Inc., Publishers, 1979, pp. 83-88.

33. "AFL-CIO Official Finds Career Ed Paper 'Atrocius'," *Education Daily.* October 1, 1973, p. 3.

34. "Why Johnny and Joann Can't Work: An Interview with Kenneth B. Hoyt", *Occupational Outlook Quarterly,* 1977, 21 (2), p. 3.

35. Hoyt, K.B. *An Introduction to Career Education: A Policy Paper of the U.S. Office of Education.* Washington, D.C.: U.S. Government Printing Office, 1975.

36. Ibid, pp. 1-2.

37. Ibid, p. 4.

38. Public Law 93-380, *Education Amendments of 1974,* August 21, 1974, 88 STAT. 553.

39. McLaughlin, D.H. *Career Education in the Public Schools 1974-75: A National Survey.* Washington, D.C.: U.S. Government Printing Office, 1976.

40. Ibid, pp. iii-iv.

41. High, S.C., Jr. "Personal Correspondence." November 29, 1980.

42. Hoyt, K.B. "Foreword" in *Career Education: A Collaborative Effort; Report on Commissioner's National Conference on Career Education.* Washington, D.C.: Dingle Associates, Inc., 1976, p. i.

43. Marland, S.P., Jr. *Career Education Update: An Address Delivered at the Commissioner's National Conference on Career Education.* Washington, D.C.: National Advisory Council for Career Education, 1976, pp. 1-3.

44. Ibid, p. 16.

45. *Career Education: A Collaborative Effort; Report on Commissioner's National Conference on Career Education.* Washington, D.C.: Dingle Associates, Inc., 1976.

46. National Advisory Council for Career Education, *Interim Report With Recommendations for Legislation.* Washington, D.C.: U.S. Government Printing Office, 1975.

47. Charek, M. *A History of the 1977 Career Education Incentive Act.* Unpublished doctoral dissertation, Southern Illinois University at Carbondale, 1979.

48. Public Law 95-207, *Career Education Incentive Act,* December 13, 1977, 91 STAT. 1464

49. Ibid, 1468.

50. Hoyt, K.B. "Strategy Considerations for Implementing the K-12 Portion of the Career Education Incentive Act." In K.B. Hoyt, *Refining the Career Education Concept: Part IV.* Washington, D.C.: U.S. Government Printing Office, 1979, p. 47.

51. Ibid, pp. 48-52.

52. High, S.C., Jr. and Hall, L. *Bibliography on Career Education.* Washington, D.C.: U.S. Office of Education, May 1973; and Hall, L. and High, S.C., Jr. *Bibliography on Career Education.* Washington, D.C.: U.S. Government Printing Office, July, 1979.

53.    Hoyt, K.B. *Career Education: Contributions to an Evolving Concept.* Salt Lake City, Utah: Olympus Publishing Company, 1975.

54.    Hoyt, K.B. *K-12 Classroom Teachers and Career Education: The Beautiful People.* Washington, D.C.: U.S. Government Printing Office, 1976.

55.    *Education & Work,* 1981, 5 (6), p. 4.

56.    *Selected Bibliography on Career Education.* Washington, D.C.: U.S. Department of Education, Division of Career Education, April 1983.

57.    Public Law 97-35, Omnibus Education Reconciliation Act of 1981, Title V of the Omnibus Budget Reconciliation Act of 1981, August 13, 1981, 95 STAT. 44.

58.    Brodinsky, B. "Something Happened: Education in the Seventies." *Phi Delta Kappan,* 1979, 61 (4), 238-241.

## BIBLIOGRAPHY

The professional literature is a very important part of the history of career education. Compiled below is a sample of the more significant books and monographs that have been written to date. They are organized into three sections. The first section was compiled by the author. The last two sections are reproduced from the 1979 *Bibliography on Career Education* from the Office of Career Education and have been updated by the author. The six digit ED number following the titles in Sections B and C refers to the ERIC accession number obtained from *Resources in Education.*

A.    **Selected Career Education Text and Reference Books.** (Limited only to those that feature career education in the title.)

1.     Bailey, L.J. and Stadt, R. *Career Education: New Approaches to Human Development.* Bloomington, Illinois: McKnight Publishing Company, 1973.

2.     Bolino, A.C. *Career Education: Contributions to Economic Growth.* New York: Praeger Publishers, 1976.

3.     Brolin, D.E. and Kokaska, C.J. *Career Education for Handicapped Children and Youth.* Columbus, Ohio: Charles E. Merrill Publishing Company, 1979.

4.     Calhoun, C.C. and Finch, A.V. *Vocational and Career Education: Concepts and Operations.* Belmont, California: Wadsworth Publishing Company, Inc., 1976.

5.     Clark, G.M. *Career Education for the Handicapped Child in the Elementary Classroom.* Denver, Colorado: Love Publishing Company, 1979.

6.     Evans, R.N., Hoyt, K.B., and Mangum, G.L. *Career Education in the Middle/Junior High School.* Salt Lake City, Utah: Olympus Publishing Company, 1973.

7.     Feldman, S.J. *Readings in Career and Vocational Education for the Handicapped.* Guilford, Connecticut: Special Learning Corporation, 1979.

8.     Fuller, J.W. and Wheaton, T.D., (Eds.) *Career Education: A Lifelong Process.* Chicago, Illinois: Nelson-Hall Inc., Publishers, 1979.

9.     Gardner, D.C. and Warren, S.A. *Careers and Disabilities: A Career Education Approach.* Stanford, Connecticut: Greylock Publishers, 1978.

10. Gillet, P. *Career Education for Children with Learning Disabilities.* San Rafael, California: Academic Therapy Publications, 1978.

11. Goldhammer, K. and Taylor, R.E., (Eds.) *Career Education: Perspective and Promise.* Columbus, Ohio: Charles E. Merrill Publishing Company, 1972.

12. Harris, N.C. and Grede, J.F. *Career Education in Colleges.* San Francisco, California: Jossey-Bass Publishers, 1977.

13. Hoyt, K.B. *Career Education: Contributions to an Evolving Concept.* Salt Lake City, Utah: Olympus Publishing Company, 1975.

14. Hoyt, K.B. *Career Education: Where It Is and Where It Is Going.* Salt Lake City, Utah: Olympus Publishing Company, 1981.

15. Hoyt, K.B., Evans, R.N., Mackin, E.F., and Mangum, G.L. *Career Education: What It Is and How To Do It. Second Edition.* Salt Lake City, Utah: Olympus Publishing Company, 1974.

16. Hoyt, K., Evans, R., Mangum, G., Bowen, E. and Gale, D. *Career Education in the High School.* Salt Lake City, Utah: Olympus Publishing Company, 1977.

17. Hoyt, K.B. and Hebeler, J.R., (Eds.) *Career Education for Gifted and Talented Students.* Salt Lake City, Utah: Olympus Publishing Company, 1974.

18. Hoyt, K.B., Pinson, N.J., Laramore, D., and Mangum, G.L. *Career Education and the Elementary School Teacher.* Salt Lake City, Utah: Olympus Publishing Company, 1973.

19. Jesser, D.L. *Career Education: A Priority of Chief State School Offices.* Salt Lake City, Utah: Olympus Publishing Company, 1976.

20. Kazanas, H.C. *Readings in Career Education.* Peoria, Illinois: Bennett Publishing Company, 1981.

21. Magisos, J.H., (Ed.) *Career Education: The Third Yearbook of the American Vocational Association.* Washington, D.C.: American Vocational Association, 1973.

22. Mangum, G.L., Becker, J.W., Coombs, G. and Marshall, P., (Eds.) *Career Education in the Academic Classroom.* Salt Lake City, Utah: Olympus Publishing Company, 1975.

23. Mangum, G.L., Gale, G.D., Olsen, M.L., Peterson, E. and Thorum, A.R. *Your Child's Career: A Guide to Home-Based Career Education.* Salt Lake City, Utah: Olympus Publishing Company, 1977.

24. Marland, S.P., Jr. *Career Education: A Proposal for Reform.* New York: McGraw-Hill Book Company, 1974.

25. McClure, L. and Buan, C., (Eds.) *Essays on Career Education.* Portland, Oregon: Northwest Regional Educational Laboratory, 1973.

26. Miller, S.R. and Schloss, P.J. *Career/Vocational Education for Handicapped Youth.* Rockville, Maryland: Aspen Systems Publication, 1982.

27. Pietrofesa, J.J., Leonard, G.E., and Giroux, R.F., (Eds.) *Career Education and the Counselor.* Washington, D.C.: American Personnel and Guidance Association, 1975.

28. Pucinski, R.C. and Hirsch, S.P., (Eds.) *The Courage to Change: New Directions for Career Education.* Englewood Cliffs, New Jersey: Prentice-Hall, Inc., 1971.

29. Reinhart, G. *Career Education: From Concept to Reality.* New York: McGraw-Hill Book Company, 1979.

30. Ressler, R. *Career Education: The New Frontier.* Worthington, Ohio: Charles A. Jones Publishing Company, 1973.

31. Stevenson, J.B. *An Introduction to Career Education.* Worthington, Ohio: Charles A. Jones Publishing Company, 1973.

32. Wigglesworth, D.C., (Ed.) *Career Education: A Reader.* San Francisco, California: Canfield Press, 1975.

B. **Monographs on Career Education.** (Issued by the Office of Career Education of the U.S. Office of Education.)

1. O'Toole, J. *The Reserve Army of the Underemployed,* 1975. (ED 109 509)

2. Chenault, J. *Career Education and Human Services,* 1975. (ED 109 507)

3. Herr, E.L. and Cramer, S.H. *Conditions in Education Calling for Reform: An Analysis,* 1975. (ED 109 508)

4. Olson, P. *The Liberal Arts and Career Education: A Look at the Past and the Future,* 1975. (ED 113 487)

5. Chenault, J. and Mermis, W. *The Professional Education of Human Services Personnel,* 1976. (ED 130 108)

6. Super, D. *Career Education and the Meanings of Work,* 1976. (ED 128 593)

7. Evans, R. *Career Education and Vocational Education: Similarities and Contrasts,* 1975. (ED 127 472)

8. Hoyt, K. *Perspectives on the Problem of Evaluation in Career Education,* 1976. (ED 127 471)

9. Hoyt, K. *K-12 Classroom Teachers and Career Education: The Beautiful People,* 1976. (ED 130 034)

10. Hoyt, K. *Application of the Concept of Career Education to Higher Education: An Idealistic Model,* 1976. (ED 130 085)

11. Hoyt, K. *Community Resources for Career Education,* 1976. (ED 130 118)

12. Hoyt, K. *Teachers and Career Education,* 1976. (ED 131 281)

13. Hoyt, K. *Refining the Career Education Concept,* 1976. (ED 132 427)

14. Hoyt, K. *Career Education for Special Populations,* 1976. (ED 132 428)

15. Hoyt, K. *Relatonships Between Career Education and Vocational Education,* 1976. (ED 132 367)

16. Hoyt, K. *Career Education Implications for Counselors,* 1977. (ED 134 821)

17. Hoyt, K. *The School Counselor and Career Education,* (ED 134 905)

18. Enderlein, T. *A Review of Career Education Evaluation Studies,* 1976. (ED 141 584)

19. Herr, E. *The British Experience in Educational Change, Careers Education, School Counselor Role and Counselor Training: Implications for American Education,* 1977. (ED 142 846)

20. Hoyt, K. *Career Education and the Business-Labor-Industry Community,* 1976. (ED 146 361)

21. Hoyt, K. *Refining the Career Education Concept: Part II,* 1977. (ED 146 362)

22. Hoyt, K. *A Primer for Career Education,* 1977. (ED 145 252)

23. Moore, C. *Baby Boom Equals Career Bust,* 1977. (ED 146 411)

24. Jackson, R. *Career Education and Minorities,* 1977. (ED 149 126)

25. Datta, L. *Career Education: What Proof Do We Have That It Works?,* 1977. (ED 151 516)

26. Preli, B. *Career Education and the Teaching/Learning Process,* 1978. (ED 164 836)

27. Hoyt, K. *Refining the Career Education Concept: Part III,* 1978. (ED 164 860)

28. Hoyt, K. *Considerations of Career Education in Postsecondary Education,* 1978. (ED 164-984)

29. Hoyt, K. *The Concept of Collaboration in Career Education,* 1978. (ED 164 861)

30. Hoyt, K. *Chambers of Commerce and Career Education,* 1978. (ED 162 158)

31. Hoyt, K. *National Alliance of Business and Career Education,* 1978. (ED 162 160)

32. Hoyt, K. *Career Education and Organized Labor,* 1978. (ED 164 983)

33. Hoyt, K. *Women's American ORT and Career Education,* 1978. (ED 164 859)

34. Hoyt, K. *4-H and Career Education,* 1978. (ED 162 159)

35. Hoyt, K. *Junior Achievement, Inc. and Career Education,* 1978 (ED 164 835)

36. Hoyt, K. *YEDPA and Career Education,* 1978. (ED 160 793; ED 194 791)

37. Hoyt, K. *Exploring Division Boy Scouts of America, Girls Scouts of the U.S.A., and Career Education,* 1978. (ED 167 806)

38. Hoyt, K. *American Legion/American Legion Auxiliary and Career Education,* 1978. (ED 167 810)

39. Hoyt, K. *Future Farmers of America and Career Education,* 1978. (ED 167 807)

40. Hoyt, K. *The National Federation of Business and Professional Women's Clubs and Career Education,* 1978. (ED 167 809)

41. Hoyt, K. *Refining the Concept of Collaboration in Career Education,* 1978. (ED 167 808)

42. Hoyt, K. *Rotary International and Career Education,* 1978. (ED 171 930)

43. Hoyt, K. *The Community Career Education Coordinator,* 1979. (ED 192 040)

44. Hoyt, K. *Community Involvement in the Implementation of Career Education,* 1979. (ED 189 315)

45.  Hoyt, K. *Funding for K-12 Career Education Efforts: Examples and Recommendations,* 1979. (ED 189 421)

46.  Hoyt, K. *Parents and Career Education: Descriptions of Current Practices,* 1979. (ED 181 304)

47.  Hoyt, K. *Refining the Career Education Concept: Part IV,* 1979. (ED 186 634)

48.  Bernstein, P. *Career Education and the Quality of Working Life,* 1980. (ED 181 295)

49.  Hoyt, K. *Evaluation of K-12 Career Education: A Status Report,* 1980. (ED 189 394)

50.  Hoyt, K. *Staff Development in K-12 Career Education,* 1980. (ED 201 824)

51.  Hoyt, K. *The Association of Junior Leagues and Career Education,* 1980. (ED 203 083)

52.  Hoyt, K. *Career Education: Retrospect and Prospect,* 1981. (ED 203 156)

53.  Hoyt, K. *LEA/Prime Sponsor Relationships: Practitioner Suggestions for Successful Solutions,* 1980. (ED 203 117)

54.  Hoyt, K. *Implementation Issues in K-12 Career Education,* 1980. (ED 209 452)

55.  *Fundamentos Basicos de Career Education,* 1980. (ED 185 372; This document is the Spanish translation of ED 145 222, *A Primer for Career Education)*

56.  Hoyt, K. *Refining the Career Education Concept: Part V,* 1980. (ED 204 603)

C.  **Publications on Career Education.** (Issued by the National Advisory Council for Career Education).

1.  National Advisory Council for Career Education. *Interim Report with Recommendations for Legislation.* November 1975. (ED-112-268)

2.  Herr, Edwin L. *The Emerging History of Career Education: A Summary View.* October 1975. (ED-122-011)

3.  Jesser, David L. *An Analysis of State Laws on Career Education and Pending State Legislation.* October 1975. (ED-122-006)

4.  Berke, Joel S. and Terry W. Hartle. *Key Concepts in Career Education: Legislative and Policy Issues.* July 1975. (ED-122-010)

5.  Berke, Joel S. and Terry W. Hartle. *Analysis and Synthesis of Existing Career Education Legislation.* 1975. (ED-122-009)

6.  Hartle, Terry W. *The Implementation and Administration of a Federal Career Education Program.* September 1975. (ED-122-008)

7.  Wasdyke, Raymond G. *Career Education and the Future.* October 1975. (ED-122-007)

8.  Worthington, Robert M. *A Review and Synthesis of Research Concerning Career Education in Doctoral Dissertations of Fellows Supported by the Education Professions Development Act, Section 552, 1972-1975.* October 1975. (ED-117-401)

9.    Smith, Keith E. *A Summary of Commissioned Papers Prepared for the National Advisory Council for Career Education.* 1976. (ED-128-661)

10.   *The Efficacy of Career Education.* 1976. (ED-130-092)

11.   National Advisory Council for Career Education. *1976 Interim Report.* (ED-141-626)

12.   National Advisory Council for Career Education. *Next Steps in Career Education.* November 1976. (ED-141-574)

13.   Marland, Sidney P., Jr. *Career Education Update.* November 1976. (ED-133-513)

14.   Sexton, Robert. *Experiential Education and Community Involvement Practices at the Postsecondary Level: Implications for Career Education.* November 1976. (ED-138-771)

15.   Rosen, David P. and others. *Masters of Reality: Certificate or Performance? Toward Policy and Practice for Postsecondary Education and Work Programs Based on Outcomes for Students.* January 1977. (ED-138-810)

16.   Goldstein, Michael B. *The Current State of Career Education at the Postsecondary Level.* June 1977. (ED-141-610)

17.   Hensley, Gene and Mark Schulman. *Two Studies on the Role of Business and Industry and Labor Participation in Career Education: Enhancing Business and Industry Participation in Career Education; Issues and Strategies for Enhancing the Participation of Labor in the Implementation of Career Education.* June 1977. (ED-141-608)

18.   Hansen, Lorraine S. *An Examination of the Definitions and Concepts of Career Education.* June 1977. (ED-141-609)

19.   Valley, John R. *Career Education of Adults.* June 1977. (ED-141-611)

20.   Katz, Martin R. and others. *The Cross-Sectional Story of Early Career Development as Revealed by the National Assessment of Educational Progress.* March 1977. (ED-147-490)

21.   Miller, Juliet V. *Career Development Needs of Nine-Year Olds: How to Improve Career Development Programs.* August 1977. (ED-147-497)

22.   Aubrey, Roger F. *Career Development Needs of Thirteen-Year Olds: How to Improve Career Development Programs.* August 1977. (ED-147-498)

23.   Mitchell, Anita M. *Career Development Needs of Seventeen-Year Olds: How to Improve Career Development Programs.* September 1977. (ED-147-555)

24.   Westbrook, Bert W. *Career Development Needs of Adults: How to Improve Career Development Programs.* August 1977. (ED-147-499)

## Chapter Three

## CAREER DEVELOPMENT NEEDS OF WOMEN

---

### Introduction

The U.S. Office of Education policy paper on career education discussed in Chapter Two, identifies eleven conditions calling for educational reform. While all eleven conditions merit attention, one has been singled out for special consideration in this chapter. It is:

> #6. The growing need for and presence of women in the work force has not been reflected adequately in either the educational or the career options typically pictured for girls enrolled in our educational system.[1]

According to Ginzberg[2], the need to devote special attention to women follows directly from the theory and practice of career guidance: (a) They are one of the groups that are most likely to be misinformed about options; (b) They lack adequate role models; and (c) Their informal informational systems are likely to be deficient. These shortcomings reflect dramatic and substantial changes in the paths that have opened up and the opportunities that lie ahead. An important role for education, guidance and counseling is to reduce the time lag between the new reality and the awareness and response to it, particularly among the present generation of young people who are making plans for the future.

### Women in the Labor Force

In present day society the term "revolution" is often used to describe social, technological, educational, or ideological change. During this century there have been revolutions in conceptions of the social, economic, and political rights of individuals; in the means of producing goods; in the kinds of services available to people and methods for providing such services; in systems of transportation; and in avenues of communication. Another extremely dramatic change has also occurred, and until quite recently, with little fanfare or recognition. This situation, once referred to by Drews[3] as a "silent revolution," is characterized by changing patterns of employment for women.

## Growth in Labor Force Participation

The actual growth in the number of women in the labor force has been phenomenal. The U.S. Department of Labor[4] reports that in 1984, 49.7 million women were in the labor force, over twice as many as in 1960. Since 1960, American women have been responsible for more than 70 percent of the total increase in the labor force and their representation in the labor force has risen from 33.4 percent to 43.6 percent of all workers. Within the population of women 16 years of age and over, the percentage of employed women advanced from 37.7 percent in 1960 to 53.6 percent in 1984. (See Table 3:1.)

Table 3:1

### WOMEN IN THE CIVILIAN LABOR FORCE*

(Women 16 years of Age and Older)

| Year | Number in Thousands | As Percent of all Workers | As Percent of Women Population |
|------|------|------|------|
| 1950 | 18,389 | 29.6 | 33.9 |
| 1955 | 20,548 | 31.6 | 35.7 |
| 1960 | 23,240 | 33.4 | 37.7 |
| 1965 | 26,200 | 35.2 | 39.3 |
| 1970 | 31,543 | 38.1 | 43.3 |
| 1975 | 37,475 | 39.9 | 46.3 |
| 1980 | 45,487 | 42.5 | 51.5 |
| 1984 | 49,709 | 43.6 | 53.6 |

Source: U.S. Department of Labor, Bureau of Labor Statistics, 1984.

* NOTE: The Department of Labor operationally defines "labor force" as encompassing those people who are "employed" and those who are "unemployed." By unemployed they mean people who are laid off or those actively looking for a job. For example, in 1984 there were 45.9 million employed women and 3.8 million unemployed women for a total of 49.7 million women in the civilian labor force. There were about 140 thousand additional women in the Armed Forces.

In addition to greater labor force participation by women, there has also been a shift in the age group showing the greatest increase. Since 1960, increases in rates of labor force participation have not been quite as rapid for women aged 45 and older, while the group aged 25 to 34 has been expanding its work role very energetically (see Table 3:2). Women 25 to 34 years old accounted for about half the increase in the number of female workers during the 1970s. A remarkable 69.3 percent of all women 25 to 34 were working in July 1983, including about 55 percent of the mothers in this age group who had to juggle the responsibilities of home and child care with those of a job. This age group is now the highest for any age group accounting for 28.6 percent of all working women (see Table 3:3). The increase for this age group from 18.1 percent in 1970 to 28.6 percent in July 1983 amounts to more than 8 million additional workers.

Table 3:2

**WOMEN IN THE CIVILIAN LABOR FORCE BY AGE**

(Annual Average as Percent of Women Within Age Group)

|  | Participation Rate (Percent of population in labor force) | | | | |
| Age | 1950 | 1960 | 1970 | 1980 | July 1983 |
| --- | --- | --- | --- | --- | --- |
| Total, 16 years and over | 33.9 | 37.7 | 43.3 | 51.5 | 52.9 |
| 16 and 17 | 30.1 | 29.1 | 34.9 | 43.6 | 38.1 |
| 18 and 19 | 51.3 | 50.9 | 53.6 | 61.9 | 62.1 |
| 20 to 24 | 46.0 | 46.1 | 57.7 | 68.9 | 69.9 |
| 25 to 34 | 34.0 | 36.0 | 45.0 | 65.5 | 69.3 |
| 35 to 44 | 39.1 | 43.4 | 51.1 | 65.5 | 68.8 |
| 45 to 54 | 37.9 | 49.8 | 54.4 | 59.9 | 62.2 |
| 55 to 64 | 27.0 | 37.2 | 43.0 | 41.3 | 41.7 |
| 65 and over | 9.0 | 10.8 | 9.7 | 8.1 | 7.6 |

Source: U.S. Department of Labor, Bureau of Labor Statistics, 1983.

The increase in labor force participation rates of women has occurred alongside a decline in the participation rates for men. During the period 1950-1980, the annual percent of employed men dropped from 86.4 percent to 77.2 percent. During this 30-year period, the number of women workers increased by 25.7 million compared to only 15.9 million for men. The percentage decline for men reflects, in part, the spread and liberalization of pension, disability, and retirement plans, and changing social attitudes toward work and lesiure. That the rates for women have risen in the presence of some of these same forces attests to the strength and durability of the movement of women into the labor force.[5]

Table 3:3

### WOMEN IN THE CIVILIAN LABOR FORCE BY AGE

(Annual Average as Percent of Total Women Workers)

| Age | 1950 | 1960 | 1970 | 1980 | July, 1983 |
|---|---|---|---|---|---|
| Total: Number (in thousands) | 18,389 | 23,240 | 31,543 | 45,487 | 48,532 |
| Percent | 100.0 | 100.0 | 100.0 | 100.0 | 100.0 |
| 16 and 17 | 3.3 | 3.5 | 4.2 | 4.0 | 2.8 |
| 18 to 19 | 6.0 | 5.4 | 6.1 | 5.7 | 5.1 |
| 20 to 24 | 14.5 | 11.1 | 15.5 | 16.0 | 15.4 |
| 25 to 34 | 22.3 | 17.8 | 18.1 | 27.0 | 28.6 |
| 35 to 44 | 22.6 | 22.8 | 18.9 | 18.9 | 21.1 |
| 45 to 54 | 18.1 | 22.7 | 20.7 | 15.4 | 14.7 |
| 55 to 64 | 10.0 | 12.8 | 13.2 | 10.3 | 10.1 |
| 65 and over | 3.2 | 3.9 | 3.4 | 2.6 | 2.4 |
| Median age | 36.7 | 40.4 | 37.8 | 34.0 | 34.4 |

Source: U.S. Department of Labor, Bureau of Labor Statistics, 1983.

## Reasons for Increased Employment

The tremendous rise in the number and proportion of women in the labor force is due to a combination of demographic, economic, educational and social developments. Following are summaries of the primary reasons.

*Financial.* Women consistently rank financial reasons as being the strongest motivator for working. The majority of women workers are either single, divorced, widowed, separated or married to men earning an inadequate family income. Thus, women work to support themselves or to raise the family's general standard of living.

*Health and Longevity.* For a woman born in 1920 the life expectancy was 55 years, but for a woman born in 1980 the life expectancy was closer to 80 years. The same factors that have extended the lifespan have reduced the incidence of disease and have given women greater vitality for fuller enjoyment of their added years. Many more women are choosing to spend these added years in paid employment.

*Marriage and Family.* Larger proportions of young women are choosing to remain single, or at least to delay marriage for a longer period of time. The percentage of married women over the age of 18 dropped from 70.9 percent in 1950 to 62.4 percent in 1981.[6] The general availability and efficiency of birth control methods and abortion by choice (an estimated 1.6 million legal abortions were performed in 1980)[7] have resulted in women being able to exercise greater control over childbearing. As a consequence, women are having fewer children and are also planning for children in a way that allows them to more easily integrate homemaking and employment.

While fewer women are marrying today, more and more are being divorced. From 1950 to 1979, the divorce rate in the United States accelerated from 2.6 to 5.4 per 1,000 population.[8] In 1981, divorced, separated, widowed, and never-married women headed 9.1 million families, representing one out of every seven of the 60.3 million families in the United States.[9]

*Educational Level.* A woman's level of formal education and her presence in the labor force are closely related. Stated simply, the more education a woman has, the more likely she is to work. In 1979, about 23 percent of women who had eight years or less of formal education were employed. For high school graduates, 57 percent were employed. And for those who graduated from college, 67 percent were employed. For college graduates who were single or divorced, the employment rate was about 85 percent.[10]

*Social and Occupational.* Two significant changes during this century have effected the employment of women. One is the shift from rural to urban households resulting in more available time for women than the former role of farm wife demanded. Another is the evolution from a primarily goods-producing economy to a service-producing economy. Currently, about two of every three workers are employed in service type industries. The relevant point here is that service-oriented fields typically employ high proportions of women workers. In July 1982, 83.4 percent of employed women were in service-producing jobs.[11]

*Technological.* The time and physical effort required for homemaking chores have been considerably reduced because of supermarkets and convenience foods; ready-made clothing and easy-care fabrics; and labor-saving appliances like automatic washers and dryers, dishwashers, garbage disposals and microwave ovens. These together with smaller families and other changes noted above have given women more time available for employment outside the home.

*Values and Life Styles.* In the last decade or so, women have been encouraged to consider how their interests, abilities and values can be more fully expressed. For some, this self-realization will be achieved primarily through marriage, home and family; for others, it will include work in addition to or in place of marriage, home and family. Larger numbers of women are now by choice devoting themselves to work because of the satisfactions and rewards they derive from it. Not unrelated is the fact that many men have also changed their values by way of encouraging and supporting working women.

*Affirmative Action.* Most of the legal barriers that previously limited women's access to and advancement in employment have now been eliminated. These are discussed more fully in a later part of this chapter.

## Under-utilization of Women Workers

The energy, talent and abilities of women are one of the nation's greatest resources. These resources are being used more fully and more creatively than ever before. During the period 1972 to 1981 increases in female labor force participation occurred for ten of the twelve occupational groups shown in Table 3:4. The largest percentage increase was for the managers and administrators group (from 17.6 to 27.5). With respect to specific occupations, an increase of 15 percentage points or more was made for accountants, personnel and labor relations workers, bank officers and financial managers, office managers, compositors and typesetters. Another two dozen occupations had increases of 10 to 14 percentage points.

Despite substantial gains made by women in a number of selected occupations, it is still a long way to the satisfactory realization of women's potential contributions. The fact remains that women continue to be concentrated in the relatively less skilled, less rewarded, and less rewarding fields of work. In 1981, about 25.2 out of a total of 43.0 million employed women (59 percent) were in the three occupational groups of clerical and kindred workers, service workers, and sales workers. Of the approximately 11.7 million women who were added to the workforce between 1972 and 1981, 6.7 million (57 percent) entered the three fields of clerical, service, and sales. Thus, even though more and more women are entering fields long dominated by men, the fact remains that the majority of women continue to enter and to work in the so-called "pink collar" occupations.

Career Education for Teachers and Counselors

Table 3:4

EMPLOYMENT OF WOMEN IN SELECTED OCCUPATIONS: 1972 AND 1981

*(Numbers Employed in Thousands)*

| Occupation | 1972 | | 1981 | |
|---|---|---|---|---|
| | Total Employed | Percent | Total Employed | Percent |
| Total . . . . . . . . . . . . . . . . . . . . . . | 82,153 | 38.0 | 100,397 | 42.8 |
| 1. Professional, technical, and kindred workers[1] . | 11,538 | 39.3 | 16,420 | 44.6 |
| Accountants . . . . . . . . . . . . . . . . . . . | 720 | 21.7 | 1,126 | 38.5 |
| Computer specialists . . . . . . . . . . . . . . . | 2.76 | 16.8 | 627 | 27.1 |
| Engineers[1] . . . . . . . . . . . . . . . . . . . | 1,111 | .8 | 1,537 | 4.4 |
| Civil . . . . . . . . . . . . . . . . . . . . . | 156 | .6 | 190 | 1.6 |
| Electrical and electronic . . . . . . . . . . . | 289 | .7 | 380 | 3.9 |
| Industrial . . . . . . . . . . . . . . . . . . | 171 | 2.4 | 237 | 11.4 |
| Mechanical . . . . . . . . . . . . . . . . . . | 192 | — — | 252 | 2.8 |
| Lawyers and judges . . . . . . . . . . . . . . . | 322 | 3.8 | 581 | 14.1 |
| Librarians, archivists, and curators . . . . . . . . | 158 | 81.6 | 192 | 82.8 |
| Life and physical scientists . . . . . . . . . . . | 232 | 10.0 | 311 | 21.9 |
| Chemists . . . . . . . . . . . . . . . . . . . . . | 120 | 10.1 | 138 | 21.7 |
| Personnel and labor relations workers . . . . . . | 312 | 31.0 | 441 | 49.9 |
| Physicians, dentists, and related practitioners[1] . . | 630 | 9.3 | 828 | 14.4 |
| Dentists . . . . . . . . . . . . . . . . . . . . | 108 | 1.9 | 130 | 4.6 |
| Pharmacists . . . . . . . . . . . . . . . . . . . | 127 | 12.7 | 152 | 25.7 |
| Physicians, medical and osteopath . . . . . . | 332 | 10.1 | 454 | 13.7 |
| Registered nurses, dietitions, and therapists[1] . . . | 956 | 92.6 | 1,654 | 92.6 |
| Registered nurses . . . . . . . . . . . . . . . | 807 | 97.6 | 1,339 | 96.8 |
| Therapists . . . . . . . . . . . . . . . . . . | 117 | 59.1 | 251 | 70.5 |
| Health technologies and technicians . . . . . . . | 319 | 69.5 | 643 | 72.3 |
| Religious workers . . . . . . . . . . . . . . . . | 293 | 11.0 | 337 | 11.9 |
| Social scientists . . . . . . . . . . . . . . . . . | 143 | 21.3 | 314 | 33.8 |
| Social and recreation workers . . . . . . . . . . | 356 | 55.1 | 511 | 62.4 |
| Teachers, college and university . . . . . . . . | 464 | 28.0 | 585 | 35.2 |
| Teachers, except college and university[1] . . . . . | 2,852 | 70.0 | 3,197 | 70.6 |
| Elemenatry . . . . . . . . . . . . . . . . . . | 1,256 | 85.1 | 1,412 | 83.6 |
| Pre-kindergarten and kindergarten . . . . . . . | 189 | 96.8 | 245 | 98.4 |
| Secondary . . . . . . . . . . . . . . . . . . . | 1,118 | 49.6 | 1,231 | 51.3 |
| Engineering and science technicians[1] . . . . . . | 835 | 9.1 | 1.141 | 18.8 |
| Drafters . . . . . . . . . . . . . . . . . . . . | 288 | 6.3 | 343 | 19.2 |
| Electrical & electronic engineering technicians | 166 | 5.5 | 275 | 11.3 |
| Technicians, except health, engineering, & science | 153 | 11.2 | 219 | 22.4 |
| Vocational and educational counselors . . . . . . | 134 | 50.0 | 188 | 53.7 |
| Writers, artists, and entertainers[1] . . . . . . . . . | 903 | 31.7 | 1,388 | 39.8 |
| Athletes and kindred workers . . . . . . . . . . | 79 | 30.8 | 135 | 43.0 |
| Editors and reporters . . . . . . . . . . . . . | 164 | 41.4 | 205 | 50.2 |
| Research workers, not specified . . . . . . . . . | 87 | 27.9 | 193 | 38.9 |
| 2. Managers and administrators, except farm[1] . . | 8,081 | 17.6 | 11,540 | 27.5 |
| Bank officers and financial managers . . . . . . . | 430 | 19.0 | 696 | 37.5 |
| Buyers, wholesale and retail trade . . . . . . . . | 162 | 32.9 | 195 | 43.6 |
| Health administrators . . . . . . . . . . . . . . | 119 | 46.6 | 219 | 49.8 |

Table 3:4 - *continued*

| Occupation | 1972 | | 1981 | |
|---|---|---|---|---|
| | Total Employed | Percent | Total Employed | Percent |
| Managers and superintendents, building . . . . . . | 137 | 42.6 | 161 | 50.9 |
| Office managers, n.e.c. . . . . . . . . . . . . . . . | 317 | 41.9 | 504 | 70.6 |
| Officials and administrators, public adminis- | | | | |
| tration, n.e.c. . . . . . . . . . . . . . . . . . . | 311 | 20.4 | 476 | 29.0 |
| Purchasing agents and buyers, n.e.c. . . . . . . . . | 366 | 21.2 | 264 | 30.3 |
| Restaurant, cafeteria, and bar managers . . . . . . | 498 | 32.4 | 727 | 40.3 |
| Sales managers . . . . . . . . . . . . . . . . . . . | 574 | 15.7 | 720 | 26.5 |
| School administrators . . . . . . . . . . . . . . . | 304 | 26.0 | 430 | 36.3 |
| 3. Sales workers[1] . . . . . . . . . . . . . . . . | 5,383 | 41.6 | 6,425 | 45.4 |
| Hucksters and peddlers . . . . . . . . . . . . . . | 231 | 73.0 | 170 | 79.4 |
| Insurance agents, brokers, and underwriters . . . | 443 | 11.6 | 595 | 23.9 |
| Real estate agents and brokers . . . . . . . . . . | 352 | 36.7 | 562 | 49.8 |
| Stock and bond sales agents . . . . . . . . . . . . | 102 | 9.9 | 159 | 17.0 |
| Sales representatives, manufacturing industries . . | 401 | 6.8 | 416 | 20.0 |
| Sales clerks, retail trade . . . . . . . . . . . . . | 2,359 | 68.9 | 2,431 | 71.2 |
| Salesworkers, except clerks, retail trade . . . . . . | 432 | 13.0 | 525 | 19.6 |
| Salesworkers, services and construction . . . . . . | 137 | 29.4 | 241 | 43.2 |
| 4. Clerical and kindred workers[1] . . . . . . . . | 14,329 | 75.6 | 18,564 | 80.5 |
| Bank tellers . . . . . . . . . . . . . . . . . . . . | 290 | 87.5 | 569 | 93.5 |
| Billing clerks . . . . . . . . . . . . . . . . . . . | 149 | 84.6 | 153 | 88.2 |
| Bookkeepers . . . . . . . . . . . . . . . . . . . . | 1,592 | 87.9 | 1,961 | 91.1 |
| Cashiers . . . . . . . . . . . . . . . . . . . . . . | 998 | 86.6 | 1,660 | 86.2 |
| Clerical supervisors, n.e.c. . . . . . . . . . . . . | 200 | 57.8 | 250 | 70.8 |
| Counter clerks, except food . . . . . . . . . . . . | 331 | 73.9 | 360 | 76.4 |
| Estimators and investigators, n.e.c. . . . . . . . . | 350 | 43.4 | 540 | 54.6 |
| File clerks . . . . . . . . . . . . . . . . . . . . . | 274 | 84.9 | 315 | 83.8 |
| Insurance adjusters, examiners, and investigators | 109 | 34.3 | 191 | 58.1 |
| Mail carriers, post office . . . . . . . . . . . . . | 271 | 6.7 | 242 | 15.7 |
| Office machine operators[1] . . . . . . . . . . . . | 679 | 71.4 | 966 | 73.6 |
|    Computer & peripheral equipment operators | 199 | 37.8 | 564 | 63.8 |
|    Key punch operators . . . . . . . . . . . . . . | 284 | 89.8 | 248 | 93.5 |
| Postal clerks . . . . . . . . . . . . . . . . . . . . | 282 | 26.7 | 269 | 37.9 |
| Receptionists . . . . . . . . . . . . . . . . . . . . | 439 | 97.0 | 675 | 97.3 |
| Secretaries . . . . . . . . . . . . . . . . . . . . . | 2,964 | 99.1 | 3,917 | 99.1 |
| Shipping and receiving clerks . . . . . . . . . . . | 453 | 14.9 | 525 | 22.5 |
| Statistical clerks . . . . . . . . . . . . . . . . . | 301 | 70.9 | 370 | 80.3 |
| Stenographers . . . . . . . . . . . . . . . . . . . | 125 | 90.4 | 74 | 85.1 |
| Stock clerks and storekeepers . . . . . . . . . . . | 513 | 22.9 | 528 | 34.8 |
| Telephone operators . . . . . . . . . . . . . . . . | 394 | 96.7 | 308 | 92.9 |
| Typists . . . . . . . . . . . . . . . . . . . . . . . | 1,025 | 96.1 | 1,031 | 96.3 |
| 5. Craft and kindred workers . . . . . . . . . . | 10,867 | 3.6 | 12,662 | 6.3 |
| Carpenters . . . . . . . . . . . . . . . . . . . . . | 1,052 | .5 | 1,122 | 1.9 |
| Other construction craftsworkers[1] . . . . . . . . | 2,261 | .6 | 2,593 | 1.9 |
|    Brickmasons and stonemasons . . . . . . . . | 176 | — — | 422 | .5 |
|    Electricians . . . . . . . . . . . . . . . . . . | 498 | .6 | 684 | 1.6 |
|    Excavating, grading, & road machine operators | 428 | — — | 422 | .5 |

Table 3:4 - *continued*

| Occupation | 1972 Total Employed | 1972 Percent | 1981 Total Employed | 1981 Percent |
|---|---|---|---|---|
| Painters, construction and maintenance . . . . | 430 | 1.9 | 471 | 5.7 |
| Plumbers and pipe fitters . . . . . . . . . . . . | 391 | – – | 472 | .4 |
| Blue-collar workers supervisors, n.e.c. . . . . . . . | 1,419 | 6.9 | 1,816 | 11.3 |
| Machinists and jobsetters . . . . . . . . . . . . . | 473 | .6 | 668 | 4.0 |
| Metalcraft workers[1] . . . . . . . . . . . . . . . | 625 | 1.9 | 626 | 4.3 |
| Sheet metal workers and tinsmiths . . . . . . . | 150 | .7 | 157 | 3.2 |
| Tool and die makers . . . . . . . . . . . . . . | 184 | .5 | 175 | 2.3 |
| Mechanics, automobile . . . . . . . . . . . . . | 1,040 | .5 | 1,249 | .6 |
| Mechanics, except automobile[1] . . . . . . . . . | 1,746 | 1.0 | 2,159 | 2.5 |
| Air conditioning, heating, and refrigeration . | 175 | – – | 212 | .5 |
| Aircraft . . . . . . . . . . . . . . . . . . . . | 124 | – – | 123 | 3.3 |
| Heavy equipment . . . . . . . . . . . . . . . . | 719 | .7 | 1,007 | 1.8 |
| Radio and television . . . . . . . . . . . . . . | 124 | – – | 109 | 3.7 |
| Printing craftworkers[1] . . . . . . . . . . . . . . | 398 | 14.9 | 402 | 24.9 |
| Compositors and typesetters . . . . . . . . . . | 171 | 17.1 | 174 | 35.1 |
| Printing press operators . . . . . . . . . . . . | 142 | 4.9 | 166 | 11.4 |
| All other craftworkers[1] . . . . . . . . . . . . . | 1,855 | 9.4 | 2,028 | 15.3 |
| Bakers . . . . . . . . . . . . . . . . . . . . . | 115 | 28.9 | 135 | 41.5 |
| Crane, derrick, and hoist operators . . . . . . . | 150 | 1.3 | 143 | .7 |
| Electric power line and cable operators . . . . | 102 | – – | 117 | .9 |
| Stationary engineers . . . . . . . . . . . . . . | 191 | 1.1 | 182 | 1.6 |
| Telephone installers and repairers . . . . . . . | 312 | 1.9 | 326 | 9.8 |
| 6. Operatives, except transport[1] . . . . . . . . . . | 10,388 | 38.6 | 10,540 | 39.8 |
| Assemblers . . . . . . . . . . . . . . . . . . . . | 1,022 | 46.8 | 1,167 | 52.4 |
| Checkers, examiners, and inspectors, mfg. . . . . | 688 | 48.5 | 800 | 53.8 |
| Cutting operatives, n.e.c. . . . . . . . . . . . . . | 239 | 27.7 | 276 | 31.5 |
| Dressmakers and seamstresses, except factory . . | 133 | 97.0 | 117 | 97.4 |
| Garage workers and gas station attendants . . . . | 504 | 4.6 | 349 | 5.7 |
| Laundry and dry cleaning operatives, n.e.c. . . . . | 166 | 69.7 | 194 | 66.5 |
| Meat cutters and butchers, except mfg. . . . . . . | 202 | 3.5 | 178 | 8.4 |
| Mine operatives . . . . . . . . . . . . . . . . . . | 144 | .7 | 270 | 2.2 |
| Packers and wrappers, exc. meat and produce . . | 649 | 61.1 | 589 | 63.2 |
| Painters, manufactured articles . . . . . . . . . . | 179 | 14.6 | 166 | 16.9 |
| Precision machine operatives . . . . . . . . . . . | 390 | 10.0 | 352 | 12.8 |
| Punch and stamping press operatives . . . . . . . | 157 | 27.4 | 107 | 31.8 |
| Sewers and stitchers . . . . . . . . . . . . . . . | 942 | 95.8 | 807 | 96.0 |
| Textile operatives . . . . . . . . . . . . . . . . . | 426 | 55.2 | 300 | 61.0 |
| Welders and flame cutters . . . . . . . . . . . . . | 558 | 3.6 | 728 | 4.7 |
| Machine operatives . . . . . . . . . . . . . . . . | 1,573 | 27.0 | 1,655 | 28.5 |
| 7. Transport equipment operatives[1] . . . . . . . | 3,223 | 4.2 | 3,476 | 8.9 |
| Bus drivers . . . . . . . . . . . . . . . . . . . . | 253 | 34.1 | 360 | 47.2 |
| Delivery and route workers . . . . . . . . . . . . | 895 | 2.5 | 563 | 8.5 |
| Fork lift and tow motor operatives . . . . . . . . | 304 | 1.0 | 369 | 5.7 |
| Taxicab drivers and chauffeurs . . . . . . . . . . | 167 | 9.0 | 164 | 9.8 |
| Truck drivers . . . . . . . . . . . . . . . . . . . | 1,449 | .6 | 1,878 | 2.7 |

**Table 3:4** - *continued*

| Occupation | 1972 | | 1981 | |
|---|---|---|---|---|
| | Total Employed | Percent | Total Employed | Percent |
| 8. Laborers, except farm[1] . . . . . . . . . . . . | 4,242 | 6.0 | 4,583 | 11.5 |
| Construction laborers, including carpenters' | | | | |
| helpers . . . . . . . . . . . . . . . . . . . . | 948 | .5 | 825 | 2.2 |
| Freight and material handlers . . . . . . . . . . . | 765 | 5.9 | 753 | 9.7 |
| Gardeners and groundskeepers, except farm . . . | 548 | 2.2 | 666 | 4.7 |
| Stockhandlers . . . . . . . . . . . . . . . . . . . | 728 | 16.9 | 992 | 24.6 |
| | | | | |
| 9. Farmers and farm managers . . . . . . . . . . | 1,690 | 5.9 | 1,485 | 11.3 |
| 10. Farm laborers and supervisors[1] . . . . . . . . | 1,386 | 32.1 | 1,264 | 25.5 |
| Farm laborers, wage workers . . . . . . . . . . . | 892 | 15.3 | 969 | 15.9 |
| Farm laborers, unpaid family workers . . . . . . . | 455 | 66.8 | 254 | 65.0 |
| | | | | |
| 11. Service workers, except private household . . | 9,584 | 57.0 | 12,391 | 59.2 |
| Cleaning service workers . . . . . . . . . . . . . . | 2,084 | 32.8 | 2,489 | 38.6 |
| Food service workers[1] . . . . . . . . . . . . . . . | 3,286 | 69.8 | 4,682 | 66.2 |
| Cooks, except private household . . . . . . . . | 873 | 62.2 | 1,393 | 51.9 |
| Waiters . . . . . . . . . . . . . . . . . . . . . | 1,132 | 91.8 | 1,477 | 89.3 |
| | | | | |
| Health service workers[1] . . . . . . . . . . . . . . | 1,513 | 87.0 | 1,995 | 89.2 |
| Health aides, except nursing, and trainees . . . | 158 | 79.6 | 317 | 84.2 |
| Nursing aides, orderlies, and attendants . . . . | 915 | 83.4 | 1,131 | 86.6 |
| Practical nurses . . . . . . . . . . . . . . . . . | 345 | 96.5 | 403 | 97.8 |
| | | | | |
| Personal service workers[1] . . . . . . . . . . . . . | 1,551 | 71.5 | 1,766 | 76.0 |
| Barbers . . . . . . . . . . . . . . . . . . . . . | 157 | 4.5 | 107 | 16.8 |
| Child care workers, except private household . | 358 | 95.8 | 426 | 95.5 |
| Hairdressers and cosmetologists . . . . . . . . | 501 | 91.2 | 577 | 89.3 |
| Protective service workers[1] . . . . . . . . . . . . | 1,150 | 5.7 | 1,459 | 10.1 |
| Firefighters . . . . . . . . . . . . . . . . . . . | 201 | .5 | 214 | .9 |
| Guards . . . . . . . . . . . . . . . . . . . . . . | 415 | 4.6 | 607 | 13.7 |
| Police and detectives . . . . . . . . . . . . . . | 418 | 2.6 | 512 | 5.7 |
| | | | | |
| 12. Private household workers[1] . . . . . . . . . . | 1,442 | 97.6 | 1,047 | 96.5 |
| Child care workers . . . . . . . . . . . . . . . . | 545 | 98.0 | 451 | 97.6 |
| Cleaners and servants . . . . . . . . . . . . . . | 715 | 97.2 | 468 | 95.1 |

[1] Includes occupations not shown separately
"n.e.c." means not elsewhere classified

Source: *Statistical Abstract of the United States: 1982-83* (103rd Edition).

The differences between men and women with respect to salaries are also a matter for deep concern. The previous discussion made obvious the fact that women are concentrated in the lower-paying occupations. Less well-known, and much more serious, is the fact that women receive substantially less pay for equal work. Women who worked at year-round full-time jobs in 1981 earned about 64 cents for every dollar earned by men.[12] For example, in 1981 men's median weekly earnings were $347 compared to $224 for women. (This gap would probably have been even wider had there not been such high levels of male unemployment during 1981 in the goods-producing industries.) This means that women had to work nearly eight days to gross the same earnings that men grossed in five days. And, this differential in earnings has remained essentially unchanged since 1955. Two primary factors have sustained the gap.[13] "First, despite the fact that increasing numbers of women are securing higher level and better paying positions, the majority are still concentrated in lower paying occupations of a traditional nature which provide limited opportunity for advancement. Second, the recent dynamic rise in women's labor force participation has resulted in larger proportions of women who are in or near the entry levels."

The real meaning of this wage gap is to recall that the majority of women work because of economic necessity. In 1980, the median income for families maintained by women was $9,160 compared to a median income of $15,650 for families maintained by men and $21,450 for married-couple families.[14] For those families maintained by women, 39.1 percent were living below the poverty level in 1980.

## Clarifying the Issues

Many of the impediments to acceptance of women in the labor force result from lack of information and understanding. Following are condensations of the major emotional issues.[15]

| The Myth | The Reality |
|---|---|
| A woman's place is in the home. | Homemaking is no longer a full-time job. Goods and services formerly produced in the home are now commercially available; laborsaving devices have lightened or eliminated much work around the home. |
| Women are not seriously attached to the labor force; they work only for "pin money." | Of the 45.9 million women employed in 1984, the majority were working because of pressing economic need. They were either single, widowed, di- |

vorced, or separated or had husbands earning an income inadequate to support their family.

Women are out ill more than male workers; they cost the company more.

Data for 1980 shows little difference in the absentee rate due to illness or injury: 4.9 work-loss days per year for men compared to 5.1 work-loss days for women.

Women do not work as long or as regularly as their male co-workers; their training is costly — and largely wasted.

While it is true that many women leave work for marriage and children, this absence is only temporary for the majority of them. They return when the children are in school. Despite this break in employment, the average woman worker has a worklife expectancy of about 25 years as compared with about 43 years for the average male worker. The single woman averages over 45 years in the labor force.

Women take jobs away from men; in fact, they ought to quit those jobs they now hold.

There were 44.2 million women employed in July 1983. The number of unemployed men was about 6.2 million. If all the women stayed home and the unemployed men were placed in the jobs held by women, there would be 38 million unfilled jobs.

Women should stick to "women's jobs" and should not compete for "men's jobs."

Jobs, with extemely rare exceptions, are sexless. Tradition rather than job content has led to labeling certain jobs as women's and others as men's. For example, although few women work as engineers, studies show that two-thirds as many girls as boys have an aptitude for this kind of work.

Women do not want responsibility on the job; they do not want promotions or job changes which add to their load.

Relatively few women have been offered positions of responsibility. But when given these opportunities, women like men, do cope with job responsibilities in addition to personal or family responsibilities.

| The employment of mothers leads to juvenile delinquency. | Studies show that many factors must be considered when seeking the causes of juvenile delinquency. Whether or not a mother is employed does not appear to be a determining factor. These studies indicate that it is the quality of a mother's care rather than the time consumed in such care which is of major significance. |
| Men do not like to work for women supervisors. | Most men who complain about women supervisors have never worked for a woman. |

## Toward Equal Education and Employment of Women

Many of the inequities related to the employment of women that are apparent in the previous section have resulted from the effects of various state and federal laws. As Simpson noted,[16] some laws that were originally intended to "protect" women against discrimination have become needlessly discriminatory. Following is a brief summary of recent federal legislation and policies that are designed to eliminate discrimination "under the law."[17] There is considerable overlap between laws that apply to discrimination in education and in employment.

*Equal Pay Act of 1963,* prohibits employers from discriminating on the basis of sex in the payment of wages for equal work on jobs requiring equal skill, effort, and responsibility and which are performed under similar working conditions.

*Civil Rights Act of 1964,* Title VII, prohibits discrimination in private employment based on sex as well as on race, color, religion, and national origin in industries affecting commerce. In March 1972, this Title was extended to cover employees of all educational institutions and state and local governments, members of labor organizations, and users of employment services.

*Executive Order 11246* (September 29, 1965), forbids discrimination by federal contractors on the bases of race, color, religion, or national origin.

*Executive Order 11375* (October 13, 1967) , amended E.O. 11246 to explicitly prohibit discrimination on the basis of sex.

*Executive Order 11478* (August 8, 1969), took additional steps to strengthen and assure equal employment opportunities. Personnel policies and practices were extended to include not only employment, but also recruitment, development, and advancement of all federal government employees.

*"Order No. 4,"* issued by former Secretary of Labor George P. Schultz on February 5, 1970, required federal contractors to establish affirmative action programs relating to the employment of minorities and women. Supplemental guidelines relating to sex discrimination were published in the *Federal Register* on June 9, 1970.

*"Revised Order No. 4"* was published in the Federal Register on December 4, 1971. The order outlines new requirements to correct the "under-utilization" of women. Efforts are required to correct any and all deficiencies in the employment of women at all levels and in all segments of the workforce.

*Public Health Service Act, Title VII and Title VIII* (1971), prohibits discrimination on the basis of sex in admissions and employment practices at educational institutions receiving grants, loan guarantees, interest subsidies or contracts available under this Act.

*Education Amendments of 1972, Title IX,* prohibits discrimination on the basis of sex in employment, admissions and treatment of all employees and students in all educational institutions receiving federal funds, grants, loans, or contracts.

*Women's Educational Equity Act* (1974), authorizes the Secretary of Health, Education and Welfare to make grants to develop non-sexist curriculum and texts, non-discriminatory vocational and other programs to achieve educational equity for all students, regardless of sex.

*Education Amendments of 1976, Title II,* requires that each state's plan for vocational education include a description of policies and procedures which the state will follow to overcome sex bias and sex stereotyping in vocational education programs. Many other provisions are also included in the legislation to aid the development of materials and programs and to provide services designed to expand women's career horizons.

*Comprehensive Employment and Training Act,* as amended in 1978, Section 132 (a), prohibits discrimination on the basis of race, color, religion, sex, national origin, age, handicap, or political affiliation or belief in programs funded under CETA.

*Job Training Partnership Act* (1982), Section 167 provides that no individual shall be excluded from participation, denied the benefits of, subjected to discrimination under, or denied employment in the administration of or in connection with any JTPA program because of race, color, religion, sex, national origin, age, handicap, or political affiliation or belief.

Decades of struggle by women's groups and sympathizers culminated in Senate passage of the Equal Rights Amendment (ERA) to the United States Constitution on March 22, 1972.[18] The major paragraph states: "Equality of rights under the law shall not be denied or abridged by the United States or any state on account of sex."

The rationale for passage of the amendment was to provide constitutional protection against laws and official practices that treat men and women differently. The mechanism to afford equality of rights for men and women is already embodied in the Fifth and Fourteenth Amendments. However, the Supreme Court has never ruled favorably to extend the "due process" provision of the Fifth Amendment or the "equal protection" concept of the Fourteenth Amendment to protection against sex discrimination. If ratified by the states, the equal rights amendment would assure the rights of all persons to *equal treatment under the law* without distinction according to sex.

When Congress passed the Equal Rights Amendment in 1972, the states were given seven years to ratify it. By March 22, 1979, only 35 of the necessary 38 states had voted in favor of it. Despite considerable opposition, Congress in the Fall of 1978 passed legislation to extend the ratification deadline to June 30, 1982. Even with the extension, however, no additional states voted to ratify it and the amendment died after a ten year struggle.

Efforts are already underway to attempt a second ratification drive. Regardless of whether the ERA eventually passes, however, there are already a number of strong, legal protections in place to assure women protection against sex discrimination in education and employment.

## Career Development of Women

The growth in female labor force participation has been accompanied by increased efforts on the part of psychologists to understand better the nature of women's career development. Career development is a term used to describe the body of theory and research which focuses on understanding *how* individuals choose occupations and *why* they select and eventually enter different occupations.[19] The literature on the subject of career development is voluminous. However, refer to Chapter Four in Herr and Cramer[20] for a good, recent summary discussion.

Traditionally, career development theorists have not distinguished between sexes, and empirical tests of theory have been limited almost entirely to boys and men. Two sociologists, Theodore Caplow and Lowell Carr, were among the first (in 1954) to point out the necessity for studying the vocational development of women apart from that of men. According to Caplow,[21] "occupational inequality is guaranteed by customs and folkways [and] differentiates the career of women apart from those of men." He then went on to list several "special conditions" that should be considered in examination of female employment.

Psathas, in a 1968 article entitled "Toward a Theory of Occupational Choice for Women"[22] examined then current theories of career development noting strengths and weaknesses of each. He did not attempt to develop a theory of occupational choice for women but rather chose to describe the factors which appeared to influence women's roles. His thesis was that an understanding of the factors which influence entry of women into occupational roles must begin with the relationship between sex role and occupational role. That is, maternity and childbearing responsibilities as biologically established and socially defined have tremendous effects in differentiating male and female occupational choices and career patterns. Psathas' article was significant in helping to call attention to the need for more adequate theories.

In 1969, Zytowski[23] proposed a theory of career development explicitly for women. He offered a series of nine postulates in an attempt to characterize the distinctive differences in the work life of men and women, their patterns of vocational participation, and the determinants of these patterns. His postulates were in large part combinations and refinements of what was already known, with a few new observations about the characteristics and behavior of women. They follow:

1. The modal life role for women is described as that of the home-maker.

2. The nature of the women's role is not static: It will ultimately bear no distinction from that of men.

3. The life role of women is orderly and developmental, and may be divided into sequences according to the preeminent task in each.

4. Vocational and homemaker participation are largely mutually exclusive. Vocational participation constitutes departure from the homemaker role.

5. Three aspects of vocational participation are sufficient to distinguish patterns of vocational participation: age or ages of entry; span of participation; and degree of participation.

6. The degree of vocational participation represented by a given occupation is defined as the proportion of men to the total workers employed in the performance of that job.

7. Women's vocational patterns may be distinguished in terms of three levels, derived from the combination of entry age(s), span, and degree of participation, forming an ordinal scale.

8. Women's preference for a pattern of vocational participation is an internal event, and is accounted for by motivational factors.

9. The pattern of vocational participation is determined jointly by preference (representing motivation) and by external, situational and environmental, and internal, such as ability, factors.

During the 1970s, the literature and research on women's career development steadily grew. Good evidence for this fact is found in examining annual reviews of research published in the *Journal of Vocational Behavior*. Since 1976 the initial article in the October issue has been an interpretive summary of the literature on "Vocational Behavior and Career Development" published during the preceding year.

For the years 1975 and 1976, most of the research relating to women dealt with sex differences or sex bias in interest measurement (18 studies).[24, 25] In the 1977 review the number of studies of this type dropped to three.[26] According to Zytowski, this was apparently due to the fact that in 1977 the American Measurement in Education and Guidance (AMEG) Commission on Sex Bias in Measurement reported on changes which the publisher of 11 popular interest inventories had introduced or planned in relation to reducing sex bias. The AMEG Commission concluded that although some technical problems remained to be solved, sex bias in interest measurement had been effectively eliminated.

In 1978, the single most productive area suggested by the review as associated with the women's movement and manifested by research primarily on sex stereotyping and women's careers (twenty-six studies were reported in this review).[27] Again, in the 1979 review a majority of the studies summarized related to the general topic of "women and work."[28] More than one-third of the articles reported related to this topic. In addition to the large number of journal articles noted for 1979, five major books were also published — *Women in the U.S. Labor Force*,[29] *Sexual Harassment of Working Women: A Case of Sex Discrimination*,[30] *Working Women and Families*,[31] *The Subtle Revolution: Women at Work*,[32] and *Career and Motherhood: Struggles for a New Identity*.[33]

The review of research for 1980 did not contain a separate section related to the vocational behavior of women.[34] However, more than 30 different articles were discussed throughout the review relating to such things as sex differences in vocational development and choice, sex effects issues, the impact of sex-role stereotypes on the quality of work life, and observations related to women's roles.

One of the major categories in the review of literature for 1981 dealt with the "Vocational Behavior of Women".[35] Forty-seven articles and books were discussed in this section dealing with: The development and implementation of women's careers through middle age, females' occupational aspirations, influences on the choices of college women, women in the work force, and family and work. One of the more significant articles identified was by Auster and Auster who summarized a profile of the young women most likely to enter a nontraditional career:

1. The mother works, probably in a high-level, nontraditional occupation.

2. The father is an achievement role model and source of occupational identification for the daughter's career orientation.

3. Both parents are supportive of their daughter's career orientation, sometimes in different ways and with varying importance at different stages of their daughter's life.

4. Family socioeconomic status is high.

5. Family size is small and she is the firstborn or an "early born" among female siblings.

6. The peer group serves as a supportive influence.

7. The influence of vocational counselors is negligible.[36]

The preceding is a good example of the body of knowledge that is beginning to emerge as a result of research on women's career development.

A major disappointment of the last decade has been the failure of career development theorists to reformulate their theories taking into account the life patterns and choices of women. Tittle and Denker in a 1977 review of major theories of career development stated that ". . . to date we must conclude that theories of women's career choices are at a very early stage of development and need considerable elaboration. One of the major weaknesses of theories, even (for example) in Krumboltz's recently proposed social learning theory, is that the influence of sex-role socialization on women's career decision making is not explicitly defined."[37]

Given the amount of literature and research related to women that has been generated in the last few years, it should be possible to formulate a theory that has both scientific rigor and practical utility. The accompanying chart (see Figure 3:1) developed by Mishler and presented in Osipow's book provides a paradigm around which a new theory could be constructed. Note that the chart illustrates how women's careers are influenced by both social and individual variables and identifies some of the basic problems facing women in their career development. "Most of the difficulties women encounter seem to have a societal antecedent and are the result of social barriers to women's capacities to implement personal attributes in a career. Some of these barriers are sex-related role and occupational stereotypes which lead to such subtle psychological problems as role conflict, role overload, and fear of success. Others are more blatant, such as explicit discrimination in employment and training as a func-

Figure 3:1

PSYCHOLOGICAL ASPECTS OF WOMEN'S CAREER DEVELOPMENT

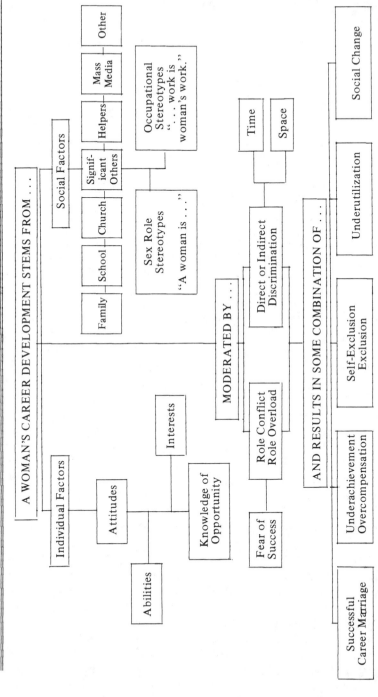

Source: S.H. Osipow (Ed.), *Emerging Women: Career Analysis and Outlooks.* Columbus, Ohio: Charles E. Merrill Publishing Co., 1975, p. 5.

tion of sex."[38] The importance of focusing attention on the subject of career development is explained by Hansen:[39]

> Concern for women's career development is not a movement to get every woman into the labor force but, rather, a concern for her uniqueness and individuality as a person and for her right to have some freedom of choice in both her personal and work life. It is concern about the overwhelmingly subordinate nature of women's roles — as nurses rather than doctors, teachers rather than principals, assembly workers rather than supervisors, secretaries rather than bosses, bank tellers rather than lending officers, administrative assistants rather than deans. It is concern about the ancillary nature of women's careers, with only small numbers, in banking, engineering, medicine, and management. It is concern about the passivity and dependence that keeps her from finding room at the top even if she has ability. It is concern about fear of competency that keeps her from maximizing her potentials and from making what Tyler (1972) has called first-class rather than second-class contributions to society. It is concern about the complexity of demands, pressures, and conflicts facing women at different life stages and the limited reward system which denies them the range of options and rewards available to men.

## The Need for Total Life Planning

The fundamental implication from knowledge of the labor force participation of women and of theories of career development, is that young women need to prepare for multiple roles during different periods in their lives. A shift has been made from the traditionally organized family where the husband is the sole breadwinner and the wife is the sole homemaker, to multiple-role families in which both partners share responsibilities for household tasks and for earning. Whereas at first multiple-role families were usually established in response to economic necessity, now more and more of these families are developed by choice.

Inevitable results of women's search for identity and for their rightful place in society are conflicts in values, needs, feelings, and situations. Figure 3:2 depicts the components which give rise to role conflicts. It is obvious that occupational decision-making for women is not a simple choice among occupational alternatives, but rather choices for a "total life plan." Total life planning cannot be completed in a short chat with a counselor during the last year of high school. But, as Bolles demonstrates in his highly successful manual for job-hunters and career changers entitled *What Color is Your Parachute?*,[40] career and life planning skills can be systematically learned and applied. Planning must be done with keen awareness of the many possibilities the years to come will bring. Following are ways in which education can aid and abet this process.

Figure 3:2

**COMPONENTS OF TOTAL LIFE PLANNING**

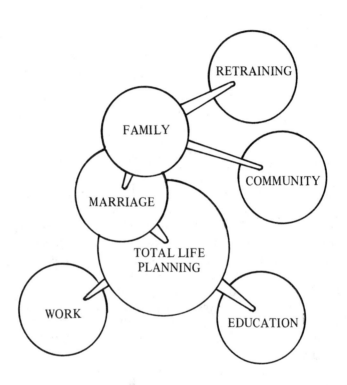

Source: U.S. Department of Labor, *Counseling Girls and Women: Awareness, Analysis, Action.* Washington, D.C.: U.S. Government Printing Office, 1966, p. 7.

## Multiple Choices and Career Patterns

It is readily apparent that women are required to make a greater number of educational, occupational, and personal decisions than men. The choice is not simply between marriage and career, but between various patternings of school, work, and marriage. Compounding the situation is the fact that choice points come much faster for a contemporary girl than they did for her mother and grandmother. "During the age period from 15 to 20 most girls take the steps and make the decisions that determine their career pattern."[41]

The initial choice which a young woman makes is a significant factor in affecting her ultimate career pattern. For example, girls who marry upon leaving or graduating from high school (these two groups encompass approximately one third of all women) who do not obtain additional education and/or work experience are almost automatically relegated to the lower paying, lower status jobs if they choose later to work. The role of career education and guidance is not to dictate personal decisions or values, but to assist girls to prepare for the dual careers of homemaking and wage earning and for interruptions in education and work. A realistic approach which does not compartmentalize girls' views of life goals is necessary. To insure that girls have requisite employability skills when they choose to enter the labor force, it is paramount that they develop such knowledges and skills *before* they leave the secondary school environment.

## Identity and Sex-Role

Traditionally, the identity issue for men has been primarily an occupational question, but for women self-definition has depended more on marriage and sex role, i.e., "Whose wife will I be, what kind of a family will we have?" Men are almost automatically assumed to become working members of society.[42] The social role expectations for girls, however, are not so clearly defined. Thus, women must make career choices on bases other than social approbation. Farmer[43] points out that the source of this conflict is not the fact that more than one role is open to women (home and career), but that a cultural lag exists between social opportunity and social sanction. Patterson[44] refers to adolescent girls as "reluctant clients" because home and family have conditioned them to accept a role definition that is no longer valid.

That society holds different definitions for the roles of men and women is made abundantly clear in the research literature and in the earlier part of this chapter on labor force participation. Education as a part of the larger society has also done its part. Taylor[45] cites examples of subtle educational practices which perpetuate sex role bias. The brainwashing many girls and women receive includes: (a) encouragement to avoid science and mathematics courses in high school; (b) almost no opportunities to choose occupational courses commonly thought of as suitable for boys; (c) advisement to lower ambitions or reconsider "unsuitable" career choices, such as engineering, veterinary medicine, or business administration; (d) evaluation against higher standards of criteria for entrance into graduate school; and (e) discrimination in the awarding of fellowships and scholarships.

To change sex role stereotypes which are as deeply ingrained as these is no easy matter. Verheyden-Hilliard[46] asks the question: "Who needs the counseling if young women are to make an effective school-to-work transition?" Her answer is that practically everyone does. Teachers, counselors, school administrators, parents, the local community, and male peers all need assistance in recognizing why girls and young women must be seen as potential adult human persons. Of course, girls and young women themselves must also be the recipients of special efforts.

Verheyden-Hilliard advocates what she calls an Affirmative Action Childhood for girls to counteract external pressures and to begin to change their view of what their lives can be. In her words:

> They need lots of on-going talk and discussion about changing women's roles, about themselves as persons of *importance, worth* and *dignity* who can be *independent* people. They needs lots of affirmative career and vocational programs. They need an educational program which recognizes the need for independence. They need support from their parents and teachers and counselors. And, where necessary, they need support to *deal* with the negative reactions of their parents, teachers, counselors, *and* boyfriends.
>
> Girls need affirmation from the day they set forth in kindergarten that it is all right for a girl to aspire to everything and that it is essential to plan to be an independent woman. Work plans should not be a patch that we rush to sew on a girl's life when she is a senior in high school.Such patchwork, however pretty and decorative, is not going to be as strong as if we had woven the design into the fabric of her life.[47]

## Opportunity for Continued Education

Successful participation in individual, dual, and interrupted career patterns is well within the capacity of most women, However, successful combinations of education, marriage and work have been difficult for women to achieve, given the present nature of education and the employment prerequisites of most jobs. Since women are not lacking for abilities and capacities, and since their contributions to society are as needed as are their contributions to families, the problem may be what Neuman describes as a question of "educational timing."[48] In simple fact, educational curricula are not set up to suit the restrictive life patterns of many women, While there are many for whom a conventional pattern of education works, there are many for whom it doesn't. The need for career education at the elementary and secondary school levels for all women, including intensive guidance and counseling, has been suggested previously. In addition, there must be accompanying adjustments in post-secondary education to permit and encourage women to continue education as times, needs, and interests permit.

Educational programs and practices designed for adolescents and young adults have proven inadequate and frustrating in many ways to more mature women who wish to continue their education. Many such women are married and have family responsibilities; many have been out of school for 10 to 20 years. A continuing education program for these women should contain the following minimum characteristics: (a) less rigid interpretation of entrance requirements, e.g., substituting equivalency tests for credit earned too long ago to be considered eligible, (b) scheduling to permit part-time attendance at hours convenient for those with young children, (c) special counseling services re both educational and occupational opportunities, (d) financial aid for those on part-time schedules, (e) and, finally, course material and teaching methods especially designed for mature women with broader backgrounds of life experience such as employment and volunteer work.

## Eliminating Sex Bias and Sex Stereotyping

Throughout the 1970s, considerable attention was given to the preparation of career education staff development materials for use by teachers and counselors in eliminating sex bias and sex stereotyping. Following are several of the more widely used resources. Each publication contains references to additional resources and instructional materials.

"Chapter Two, Sexism in Materials: How to Detect It and How To Counteract Its Effects in the Classroom." In *EPIE Career Education S\*E\*T\**, *Volume I: How to Select and Evaluate Instructional Materials.* New York: EPIE Institute, 1975.

Stebbins, L.B., Ames, N.L. and Rhodes, I. *Sex Fairness in Career Guidance: A Learning Kit.* Cambridge, Massachusetts: Abt Publications, 1975. (ED 127 462)

Peterson, M. and Vetter, L. *Sex Fairness in Career Education.* Columbus, Ohio: The ERIC Clearinghouse on Career Education, 1977. (ED 149 179)

Verheyden-Hilliard, M.E. *Reducing Sex Stereotyping in Career Education: Some Promising Approaches to Persistent Problems.* Washington, DC: U.S. Government Printing Office, May 1979. (ED 174 854)

A significant event in the continuation of efforts to promote sex equity was the National Conference on Combatting Stereotyping in Career Choice held during November 26-28, 1979 in Washington, D.C.. The Conference was conducted by the American Institutes for Research (AIR) under contract with the U.S. Office of Education. In addition to sex stereotyping, the conference was concerned with race and handicap stereotyping.

The conference dealt primarily with three topics: (a) The results of AIR's national search for successful programs designed to combat sex, race, and handicap stereotyping in career choice were reported; (b) Examples of specific programs were provided; and (c) Selected state coordinators of career education were asked to describe and discuss efforts in their individual states. The culmination of the AIR contract was the preparation and dissemination of two types of materials:

*Programs to Combat Stereotyping in Career Choice*, April 1980, 252 pp. (ED 187 886)

*Classroom Activities to Combat Stereotyping in Career Choice,* April 1980, 132 pp. (ED 187 887)

The materials were printed by the U.S. Government Printing Office and are available through the Superintendent of Documents.

The *Women's Educational Equity Act* that was included as a part of the *Education Amendments of 1974,* Section 408 provides funds to support demonstration, developmental, and dissemination activities contributing to educational equity for women and girls. Various types of instructional materials resulting from these activities are contained within a catalog entitled "Resources for Education Equity". The catalog is available from:

WEEA Publishing Center
Education Development Center, Inc.
55 Chapel Street
Newton, Massachusetts 02160

## Summary

Discussions of women's rights run the risk of becoming emotion-charged. Stereotypes of bra-burning, man-hating females are frequently brought to consciousness by mention of Women's Liberation. Major movements for political, religious, or social justice are spurred by vocal, radical elements (from either the right or the left) which frighten and alienate many people. The situation with respect to women's rights is typical. Overreaction by proponents and overreaction by opponents tends to shroud the movement's focus on its two most fundamental issues:[49] (a) The bind that women are in because of early role stereotyping which continues to be reinforced throughout their lives, preventing them from searching for alternate and/or multiple roles and from engaging in a variety of tasks; and (b) discrimination against women in education and work.

This chapter was designed to sensitize the reader to the sex equity and career development needs of girls and women. Although treatment of the subject has been brief, the situation is clear: Sexism in education and work exists and must be eliminated. Put another way, equal educational and career opportunities for women is a *matter of simple justice.*[50]

## REFERENCES

1. Hoyt, K.B. *An Introduction to Career Education: A Policy Paper of the U.S. Office of Education.* Washington, D.C.: U.S. Government Printing Office, 1975, p. 2.

2. Ginzberg, E. *Career Guidance: Who Needs It, Who Provides It, Who Can Improve It.* New York: McGraw-Hill, 1971.

3. Drews, E.M. "Counseling for Self-Actualization in Gifted Girls and Young Women." *Journal of Counseling Psychology,* 1965, 12, 167-176.

4. U.S. Department of Labor. *Perspectives on Working Women: A Databook,* Bulletin 2080, Washington, D.C.: U.S. Government Printing Office, October 1981. *Employment and Earnings.* 1983, 30(1), p. 140-141. Personal Correspondence with Bueeau of Labor Statistics, September 1983. *Employment in Perspective: Working Women,* Report 716, Bureau of Labor Statistics, Fourth Quarter, 1984.

5. U.S. Department of Labor, 1980, p. 2-3.

6. U.S. Bureau of the Census. *Statistical Abstract of the United States: 1982-83,* (103rd Edition). Washington, D.C.: U.S. Government Printing Office, 1982, p. 39.

7. Ibid, p. 68.

8. Ibid, p. 82.

9. Ibid, p. 43.

10. U.S. Department of Labor, 1980, p. 44.

11. U.S. Department of Labor, Bureau of Labor Statistics. *Employment in Perspective: Working Women,* Report 674, Third Quarter 1982.

12. U.S. Bureau of the Census, 1982, p. 404.

13. U.S. Department of Labor, *The Earnings Gap Between Women and Men.* Washington, D.C.: U.S. Government Printing Office, 1979, p. 1.

14. U.S. Department of Labor, Bureau of Labor Statistics. *Employment in Perspective: Working Women,* Report 669, Second Quarter 1982.

15. U.S. Department of Labor. *The Myth and the Reality.* Washington, D.C.: U.S. Government Printing Office, 1971. United States Department of Labor, Bureau of Labor Statistics. "The Employment Situation: August 1983," USDL 83-387, September 2, 1983. U.S. Bureau of Census, 1982.

16. Simpson, E.J. "The New Womanhood: Education for Viable Alternatives." In R.C. Pucinski and S.P. Hirsch (Eds.), *The Courage to Change: New Directions for Career Education.* Englewood Cliffs, New Jersey: Prentice-Hall, 1971, p. 59-81.

17. U.S. Department of Labor, *1969 Handbook on Women Workers.* Washington, D.C.: U.S. Government Printing Office, 1969. Stebbins, L.B., Ames, N.L. and Rhodes, I. *Sex Fairness in Career Guidance: A Learning Kit.* Cambridge, Massachusetts: Abt Associates, 1975. U.S. Department of Labor, *Employment and Training Report of the President.* Washington, D.C.: U.S. Government Printing Office, 1979; 1982; 1983.

18. Olson, C.T. "The U.S. Challenges Discrimination Against Women." *Junior College Journal,* 1972, 42(9), 13-16.

19. Crites, J.O. *Vocational Psychology.* New York: McGraw-Hill, 1969.

20. Herr, E.L. and Cramer, S.H. *Career Guidance and Counseling Through the Life Span: Systematic Approaches.* Boston: Little, Brown & Co., 1984.

21. Caplow, T. *The Sociology of Work.* Minneapolis: University of Minnesota Press, 1954.

22. Psathas, G. "Toward a Theory of Occupational Choice for Women." *Sociology and Social Research,* 1968, 52(2), 253-268.

23. Zytowski, D.G. "Toward a Theory of Career Development for Women." *Personnel and Guidance Journal,* 1969, 47, 660-664.

24. Osipow, S.H. "Vocational Behavior and Career Development, 1975: A Review." *Journal of Vocational Behavior,* 1976, 9, 129-145.

25. Betz, E.L. "Vocational Behavior and Career Development, 1976: A Review." *Journal of Vocational Behavior,* 1977, 11, 129-152.

26. Zytowski, D.G. "Vocational Behavior and Career Development, 1977: A Review." *Journal of Vocational Behavior,* 1978, 13, 141-162.

27. Walsh, W.B. "Vocational Behavior and Career Development, 1978, A Review." *Journal of Vocational Behavior,* 1979, 15, 119-154.

28. Garbin, A.P. "Vocational Behavior and Career Development, 1979: A Review." *Journal of Vocational Behavior,* 1980, 17, 125-170.

29. Cahn, A.F. (Ed.) *Women in the U.S. Labor Force.* New York: Praeger, 1979.

30. Mackinnon, C.A. *Sexual Harassment of Working Women: A Case of Sex Discrimination.* New Haven, Connecticut: Yale University Press, 1979.

31. Feinstein, K.W. *Working Women and Families.* Beverly Hills, California: Sage Publications, 1979.

32. Smith, R.E. (Ed.) *The Subtle Revolution: Women at Work.* Washington, D.C.: The Urban Institute, 1979.

33. Roland, A. & Harris, B. *Career and Motherhood: Struggles for a New Identity.* New York: Human Sciences Press, 1979.

34. Bartol, K.M. "Vocational Behavior and Career Development, 1980: A Review." *Journal of Vocational Behavior,* 1981, 19, 123-162.

35. Fretz, B.R. & Leong, T.L. "Vocational Behavior and Career Development, 1981: A Review." *Journal of Vocational Behavior,* 1982, 21, 123-163.

36. Ibid, p. 125.

37. Tittle, C.K. and Denker, E.R. "Re-Entry Women: A Selective Review of the Educational Process, Career Choice, and Interest Measurement." *Review of Educational Research,* 1977, 47, 531-584.

38. Osipow, S.H. "Introduction: Concepts in Considering Women's Careers." In S.H. Osipow (Ed.) *Emerging Women: Career Analysis and Outlooks.* Columbus, Ohio: Charles E. Merrill Publishing Company, 1975, p. 6.

39. Hansen, L.S. "Counseling and Career (Self) Development of Women." In H.J. Peters and J.C. Hansen, *Vocational Guidance and Career Development: Selected Readings,* (Third Edition). New York, MacMillan Publishing Co., 1977, p. 453-474.

40. Bolles, R. *What Color is Your Parachute?* Berkeley, California: Ten Speed Press, 1972.

41. Havighurst, R.J. "Counseling Adolescent Girls in the 1960's." *Vocational Guidance Quarterly,* 1965, 13, 153-160.

42. Neuman, R.R. "When Will the Educational Needs of Women Be Met? Some Questions for the Counselor." *Journal of Counseling Psychology,* 1963, 10, 378-383.

43. Farmer, H.S. "Helping Women to Resolve the Home-Career Conflict." *Personnel and Guidance Journal,* 1971, 49, 795-801.

44. Patterson, L.E. "Girls' Careers – Expression of Identity." *Vocational Guidance Quarterly,* 1973, 21, 269-275.

45. Taylor, E. "The Women's Movement: What It's All About." *American Vocational Journal,* 1970, 45(9), 16 & 17.

46. Verheyden-Hilliard, M.E. "Assisting the School-to-Work Transition for Young Women: Who Needs the Counseling?" In U.S. Department of Labor, *Young Women and Employment: What We Know and Need to Know About the School-to-Work Transition.* Washington, D.C.: U.S. Government Printing Office, 1978, p. 38-42.

47. Ibid, p. 41.

48. Neuman, 1963.

49. Astin, H.S., Saniewick, N. and Dweck, S. *Women: A Bibliography on Their Education and Careers.* Washington, D.C.: Human Service Press, 1971, p. 1.

50. *A Matter of Simple Justice.* The Report of the President's Task Force on Women's Rights and Responsibilities. Washington, D.C.: U.S. Government Printing Office, 1970.

4

# A DEVELOPMENTAL CURRICULUM MODEL
# FOR CAREER EDUCATION

## Introduction

A basic principle of education is: "The more important the learning outcome, the more difficult it is to state, to develop, and to evaluate." The practical meaning of this statement is, that in order for the major aims of education to be achieved (such as making a transition from school to work), they must be intelligently formulated and systematically developed and evaluated. Important learnings are seldom achieved in a haphazard, trial-and-error fashion.

A curriculum model is a plan or vehicle for identifying and organizing the learning outcomes appropriate for a particular type of education. In this chapter, a K-12 curriculum model for career education is presented and discussed. In the next chapter it will be demonstrated how the model is used to organize instructional units and to develop lesson plans.

## Purpose and Roles

Consistent with the U.S. Office of Education policy paper, career education is defined here to mean, "the totality of experiences through which one learns about and prepares to engage in work as part of her or his way of living."[1] This definition is based on a broad consensus of views from among many different types of education professionals. It is simple, concise, and clearly communicates the purpose of career education. In accomplishing this purpose, two roles need to be accomplished:

The *primary* role for career education is to facilitate concepts, attitudes, and skills related to the career development aspect of general growth and learning.

The *secondary* role for career education is to help facilitate basic academic skills through the infusion of work-related concepts and activities into academic subject areas.

These two roles are complementary, and both are equally important. However, to fail to understand the difference between the two roles, or to do one without doing the other, would be to lessen the potential for career education as a vehicle for reform. Further discussion and use of examples will help to clarify this contention.

**Primary Role: To Facilitate Career Development**

In order to comprehend the difference between the two roles for career education, it is necessary to distinguish between *ends* and *means*. The concept of ends is used to refer to the learning outcomes of education. It is synonymous with purposes, aims, goals, and objectives. All of these terms are simply different levels of learning outcomes. Means, on the other hand, refer to the topics, activities, materials, methods, curricula, etc., by which such ends are developed.

An analogy will help to illustrate this distinction. Language arts is a name for a program of instruction that is designed to facilitate the *process of communications.* What are the learning outcomes? The language arts teacher is concerned with developing concepts and skills of reading, writing, listening, speaking, and acting out (ends).

In the same way that language arts is a curriculum designed to facilitate the process of communications, career education is the name of a curriculum designed to facilitate the *process of career development.* Whereas learning outcomes (objectives) can be derived from an analysis of the construct of communication, learning outcomes can be similarly derived from an analysis of the construct of career development. (See Figure 4:1, page 94.)

**Secondary Role: To Help Facilitate Basic Academic Skills**

In this approach, teachers utilize topics, activities, materials, and methods related to "work" to infuse the conventional subject areas such as math, science, language arts and social studies. At present, this is the most common form in which career education is being implemented, especially at the elementary school level.

The teaching of basic academic skills such as reading, writing, computing, measuring, observing, using space/time relationships, drawing logical conclusions from historical events, etc., can be made more relevant and concrete through the use of "work-related" concepts and activities. Examples might include: (a) using books about occupational clusters to teach reading; (b) writing themes about "My Future Career Goals"; (c) learning to spell words associated with a

Figure 4:1

ILLUSTRATIVE CONCEPTUAL RELATIONSHIP BETWEEN LANGUAGE ARTS AND CAREER EDUCATION

| MEANS | ENDS |
|---|---|
| **Language arts** – a program of instruction (topics activities, materials) designed to facilitate the process of communications. | Concepts, attitudes and skills of:<br>1.  Reading<br>2.  Writing<br>3.  Listening<br>4.  Speaking<br>5.  Acting out. |
| **Career education** – a program of instruction (topics activities, materials) designed to facilitate the process of career development. | Concepts, attitudes and skills of:<br>1.  Self knowledge<br>2.  Occupational, educational, and economic knowledge<br>3.  Sense of agency<br>4.  Information processing and decision making<br>5.  Interpersonal relationships<br>6.  Attitudes and values toward work |

certain occupational role; (d) conducting a simulation of a super-market to help students learn computation skills; and (e) research-ing types of occupations that depend on a knowledge of science.

## Relationships Between the Two Roles

The differentiation between two roles for career education is more than a simple matter of semantics. The successful achievement of the first role will require schools to introduce and emphasize *new learning outcomes* which have not traditionally been a part of the curriculum. (Do not assume that a separate curriculum is automat-ically required.) The successful achievement of the second role only requires schools to introduce *new content and methods.* Again, ex-amples will help to clarify this distinction.

> The learner objective dealing with "Explores occupational clus-ters to validate occupational preferences and to develop new knowledge and attitudes," is an example of an important out-come for career education that is not currently being met in the majority of the nation's schools *(primary role).*

> Using a variety of materials to teach reading, however, is cur-rently being done. Using materials and methods related to work, to teach reading, may be an additional way to add interest and relevance *(secondary role).*

However, note how misleading it is to say that reading about occupations is "career education." This is akin to saying that read-ing about dinosaurs is "dinosaur education." Also, consider how lim-iting it is to view career education only as a means to facilitate basic academic skills. This can be illustrated by reference to academically talented students who have already mastered the basic skills but may have no idea of what they are going to do with their lives.

Obviously both approaches are important. Learning about and preparing for work, and developing mastery of basic academic skills are rightly inseparable. The best programs of career education will be those in which teachers combine a career development objective with another knowledge, attitude or skill objective. Different approaches to implementing career education will be discussed in Chapter Five.

## The Nature of Career Development

A fundamental tenet of curriculum development is that goals and objectives should be identified *prior* to the selection or develop-ment of content, activities and materials. Instructional components are only developed or selected in terms of the degree to which they lead to mastery of the curriculum objectives. The above introduction has pointed out the need to formulate learning outcomes for career education that are based on an understanding of the process of career development. Following is a synthesis of principles of career development which are generally acknowledged to be characteristic of the manner in which an individual develops a mature career identity.

1.  Career development is one aspect of an individual's overall pattern of growth and learning.

2.  Career development is a long-term evolutionary process, beginning in infancy and extending through adulthood.

3.  Career development is the summation of a complex series of career-related decisions made by the individual over a considerable span of time.

4.  An individual's striving to arrive at an appropriate occupational goal may be interpreted as an attempt to implement one's self-concept.

5.  Career development proceeds through a series of primarily culturally-induced developmental periods or life stages.

6.  Each developmental life stage involves meeting and coping with increasingly complex developmental tasks. The developmental tasks are susceptible to further description and elaboration.

7.  Development through the life stages can be guided. The knowledge, skills, attitudes, and motivation essential for coping with the developmental tasks can be fostered and developed. Career decision-making can be fostered and developed. Career decision-making can be done on a rational basis.

8.  The degree of mastery of a developmental task and the quality of an occupational decision is a function of the type, amount, and validity of data and experiences to which the individual has been exposed.

## About the Model

The above principles of career development have been incorporated into a curriculum model for career education which is discussed in the remainder of this chapter. The model (see Figure 4:2) is based on the concepts of *developmental stages* and *developmental tasks.* Four stages are presented in which the overall purpose of the stages is discussed. For each stage, six career developmental tasks are identified. The six tasks for each stage may be considered as the equivalent of broad educational goals (see Table 4:1). Next, sample general and specific performance objectives are stated which become the basis for developing instructional units and lessons. The reader should be aware that this curriculum model is only *one* of several different types of models which have been developed by various authors.

The motivation for developing the model was to aid local education agency personnel in organizing and implementing a systematic,

**Figure 4:2**

**A DEVELOPMENTAL CURRICULUM MODEL FOR CAREER EDUCATION**

| Types of Career Development Outcomes | A. Awareness K-3 | B. Accommodation 4-6 | C. Orientation 7-8 | D. Exploration and Preparation 9-12 |
|---|---|---|---|---|
| 1. Comprehending the nature of oneself | A1 | B1 | C1 | D1 |
| 2. Comprehending the nature of occupations, the economic system, and educational alternatives. | A2 | B2 | C2 | D2 |
| 3. Accepting responsibility for career planning | A3 | B3 | C3 | D3 |
| 4. Developing skills in information processing and decision making | A4 | B4 | C4 | D4 |
| 5. Relating to individuals and groups | A5 | B5 | C5 | D5 |
| 6. Developing attitudes and values toward work | A6 | B6 | C6 | D6 |

Table 4:1

**GOAL STATEMENTS FOR CAREER EDUCATION STAGES**

**Awareness Stage: Grades K-3**

A1.   Becoming aware of self characteristics
A2.   Becoming aware of different types of work roles
A3.   Showing awareness of responsibility for own behavior
A4.   Knowing how to organize information for learning and action
A5.   Learning cooperative social behavior
A6.   Showing interest in learning about work

**Accommodation Stage: Grades 4-6**

B1.   Developing greater self knowledge
B2.   Developing concepts about the world of work
B3.   Displaying increased responsibility for own behavior
B4.   Learning how to gather information and make decisions
B5.   Showing awareness of the nature of group membership
B6.   Accepting differences in work attitudes and values

**Orientation Stage: Grades 7 and 8**

C1.   Clarifying occupational self-concept
C2.   Surveying the structure and interrelatedness of the American economic system
C3.   Recognizing responsibility for own career planning
C4.   Practicing information-seeking and decision-making methods
C5.   Participating in simulated, group work activities
C6.   Appreciating the role of work in meeting social and individual needs

**Exploration and Preparation Stage: Grades 9-12**

D1.   Crystallizing and implementing occupational self-concept
D2.   Executing plans to qualify for post-secondary career objectives
D3.   Displaying commitment to implementation of a career plan
D4.   Demonstrating competency in decision-making skills and strategies
D5.   Demonstrating effective interpersonal skills in relation to work
D6.   Demonstrating effective work habits and attitudes

articulated career education program. It is a good, comprehensive plan. It is a valid point of departure. At the same time, it is to be expected that local teachers may choose to emphasize some goals more than others; to modify or add certain specific objectives; or to eliminate some objectives.

## Awareness Stage: Grades K-3

The period of schooling that spans the years K-3 is the child's first encounter with a formal learning environment. When a child enters the elementary school, he or she has long been displaying in recognizable form *inductive* processes of learning.[2] That is, exposure to objects through manipulation, observation, use, and so on, has led to familiarity on the basis of which the child forms generalizations about them. For example, through ordinary experience with articles in his or her environment, a child learns which things are "clothes," "foods," and "animals." Up to the age of five or six, behavior is to a large degree egocentric, i.e., determined mainly by specific experiences and activities of the child.

About the ages of six to eight the child begins to shift from *inductive* to more *deductive* behavior.[3] Awareness of concrete, perceptually known properties of and relations between objects gives way to grouping and abstract symbolic behavior. Now, the child begins to employ already formed generalizations to deal appropriately with new objects or with familiar objects in new ways. According to Formanek and Morine, growth in concept formation and cognitive development is generally brought about by the organizing of aspects of the external environment in such a way that classes of objects or concepts are formed.[4] In order to deal with the large numbers of objects in his or her world, the child must represent them in some way. This representation usually involves some form of grouping or categorizing.

Based on the above, Vinacke suggests that there are two basic curriculum considerations to be recognized in the early school years.[5]

> First, the child needs to be exposed to the ingredients of concepts. From knowledge of concrete properties of objects and their relations to each other, the child can evolve precise, stable, and complete conceptions. Second, since the child is learning how to generalize, how to symbolize, how to apply the same concept to a variety of situations, he or she needs practice and guidance in the efficient, harmonious, and productive cultivation of these skills.

The function of career education during the awareness stage thus becomes that of helping the child to perceive the ingredients which are the forerunners of more effective career development concepts and behaviors and to develop skills for differentiating and internalizing new phenomena.

### Goals and Rationale

A1. *Becoming aware of self charactedistics.* In early childhood, individuals begin the process of self concept formation which continues throughout their lives. Initially, children gather sensory impressions (i.e., "self-percepts") related to their physical configuration and their capabilities.[6] Gradually, they begin to organize their perceptions into higher-order generalizations and, finally, into simple self-concepts. That is, the impressions one receives from activities and interpersonal relationships are combined to form mental pictures. Emphasis on self-awareness and differentiation of self from others helps the child develop a repertoire of self-percepts which become the foundation for more accurate and comprehensive self-concepts.

1. Forms generalizations about self

    1.1 Provides examples to illustrate what is meant by "characteristics"

    1.2 Summarizes ways in which an individual may be described, e.g. emotions, actions, personal information, physical appearance

    1.3 Identifies own self-characteristics and attributes

    1.4 Recognizes uniqueness of own self

    1.5 Differentiates self from others

2. Understands the concept of interests

    2.1 Explains what is meant by an "interest"

    2.2 Describes how people become interested in an activity

    2.3 Identifies own interests

    2.4 Describes how people express their interests in work and play

    2.5 Relates own interests to various work activities

3. Understands the relationship between interests and occupations and leisure activities

    3.1 Explains how interests may be satisfied in a variety of occupational roles

    3.2 Infers why it is desirable to work at an occupation that one is interested in

    3.3 Explains how interests may also be expressed in leisure activities

    3.4 Illustrates how knowledge of interests helps in making decisions

**A2.** *Becoming aware of different types of work roles.* The young child perceives people performing different types of work activities, but is not able to conceptualize differences among them.[7,8] For example, children do not distinguish the work that their parents may do in an occupation outside the home from the "work" that is done within the home, or from hobby and/or volunteer activities done in addition to an occupation. This goal is closely related to A4 which is designed, in part, to help the child develop skills to make such distinctions.

1.  Examines different types of human activity

    1.1  Formulates a broad, general definition for what is "work"
    1.2  Explains what is meant by "leisure"
    1.3  Recognizes commonalities of work and leisure

2.  Differentiates types of work activities

    2.1  Defines the term "occupation"
    2.2  Describes how an occupation differs from other types of work activity
    2.3  Distinguishes among occupations, household chores, volunteer work, and leisure activity
    2.4  Associates different types of work and leisure activities with various family members
    2.5  Observes and talks to various workers in the school and neighborhood to differentiate occupational roles

3.  Understands concepts (i.e., economic groups) of goods, services, consumers, and producers

    3.1  Defines what is meant by the term "consumer"
    3.2  Understands that everyone is a consumer
    3.3  Differentiates between goods and services
    3.4  Defines what is meant by the term "producer"
    3.5  Provides examples of people who produce goods and people who produce (i.e., provide) services

4.  Understands how goods and service producers are interrelated

    4.1  Examines own family unit to understand the principle of interdependence
    4.2  Explains how specialization leads to interdependence
    4.3  Provides examples to illustrate how goods and services workers depend on each other
    4.4  Recognizes why worker cooperation is necessary in the production of goods and services
    4.5  Describes· the individual work habits and attitudes that contribute to cooperative work relationships

5.  Understands that production of most goods and services involves a "family" type of effort

    5.1  Identifies different types of job families under the broad headings of goods and services producers
    5.2  For a given occupational family (e.g., leisure, construction, health), describes types of goods produced or services provided

6.  Examines the nature of a job family (i.e., occupational group)

    6.1  Recognizes the wide range of different occupations within a single family
    6.2  Understands that many different levels exist within a job family
    6.3  Describes what is meant by the term "job ladder"
    6.4  Recognizes that individual occupations may be found in more than one job family

**A3.** *Showing awareness of responsibility for own behavior.* This goal is related to A1 in which children begin to recognize their own uniqueness, and to A2 in which they become more aware of the types of roles that they and others perform. These preceptions provide the basis for children understanding that: (a) they are responsible for their actions, and (b) they control their own actions by choosing from available alternatives. The child's development of a sense of control is seen as a prerequisite to later acceptance of responsibility for career planning.

1. Shows awareness of the consequences of own behavior
   - 1.1 Gives examples of occasions in which own behavior has made others happy and unhappy
   - 1.2 Gives examples of occasions in which own behavior has made self happy and unhappy
   - 1.3 Discusses the degree to which he/she is aware of how own actions affect self and others
   - 1.4 Discusses the following: "If someone hits you because you are teasing them, who is at fault?"

2. Shows awareness of the relationship between emotions and actions
   - 2.1 Identifies things he/she often worries about
   - 2.2 Compares own worries to those of classmates
   - 2.3 Discusses what individuals can do to deal with their worries
   - 2.4 Explains why worries often lessen, once action toward a problem has begun
   - 2.5 Discusses which is the better approach to worries — wishful thinking or positive action

3. Recognizes the potential for greater self-initiative
   - 3.1 Names things he/she now does that used to be done by parents
   - 3.2 Identifies things he/she might begin learning to do
   - 3.3 Discusses whether "success" is more related to luck or to individual effort
   - 3.4 Gives examples of occupations which require considerable individual initiative
   - 3.5 Identifies things which can be done to make own environment more as he or she would like it

**A4.** *Knowing how to organize information for learning and action.* This goal includes the development of two types of fundamental behaviors: (a) classification skills and (b) decision-making skills. With respect to the first type of behavior, research on the nature of concept formation has demonstrated that categorization ability is intimately related to children's cognitive development. Formanek and Morine conclude that "developing concepts such as 'group,' 'role,' or 'sanction' in the social sciences demands a skill in identifying similarities and differences in human behavior. Consequently, a child's ability to categorize would seem to bear some relation to his ability to understand much of the modern elementary school curriculum."[9] The implications for the understanding of occupational groups are self-evident.

The introduction to decision-making is designed to acquaint the child with the "logic" of choosing from among alternatives. While most children may not be able to conceptualize decision-making as a process, they will be able to apply such methods to the choosing of alternative courses of action, alternate behaviors, and alternate modes of expression. "From early childhood through adulthood the skills and motives needed for making wise decisions are essential elements in the equipment of the maturing person."[10]

1. Understands the characteristics of grouping systems

   1.1 Defines what is meant by a "group"
   1.2 Explains how grouping can be used to organize information
   1.3 Shows how objects, events, etc., can be classified in many different ways
   1.4 Explains how groups can be created for different purposes

2. Understands that grouping can help in organizing information about interests and occupations

   2.1 Reviews meaning of interests
   2.2 Distinguishes how an individual's specfic interests may be grouped into a number of broad areas
   2.3 Illustrates the usefulness of knowing occupations in terms of interest areas

3. Knows decision-making methods and procedures

   3.1 Describes what is meant by a "decision"
   3.2 Provides examples to illustrate decisions he/she makes daily
   3.3 Identifies steps involved in making a decision
   3.4 Distinguishes between "good" and "bad" decisions
   3.5 States why it is important to consider alternatives in making decisions
   3.6 Speculates about decisions he/she will have to make in the future

**A5.** *Learning cooperative social behavior.* Like previous goals the need for effective working relationships is a fundamental behavior of childhood that continues throughout life. As Havighurst notes, ". . . the nine- or ten-year-old clearly shows what he will be like, socially, at fifty."[11] The technique of behavior modification notwithstanding, Havighurst's observation is well-taken in that social relationships constitute a foundation element in later adaptions to life and its demands. Effective working relationships with one's peers are not some frosting on the educational cake that is desirable if it comes about incidentally. Rather, it is an essential ingredient of the cake itself.[12]

1.  Shows awareness of the importance of group cooperation

    1.1  Describes how working with others is often better and faster than working alone

    1.2  Describes how working with others may be more fun than working alone

    1.3  Differentiates between "acceptable" and "unacceptable" behavior of group members

    1.4  Discusses responsibility of each individual for making a group project successful

    1.5  Gives examples of occupations which depend on people working together

2.  Shows awareness of the logical consequences of cooperation and noncooperation

    2.1  Describes how working for one's self-interest may detract from group goals

    2.2  Describes how each person's contribution is needed to get a job done

    2.3  Illustrates how people react differently to suggestions vs. demands

3.  Participates in productive group activities

    3.1  Gains practice in group planning

    3.2  Joins in activities designed to achieve group goals

    3.3  Completes assigned tasks

    3.4  Shares in group successes and failures

    3.5  Discusses similarities between adult work groups and student work groups

**A6.** *Showing interest in learning about work.* Probably at no other time do children have as high a regard for work as they do in early childhood. The tendency for children to play at work is well-known, Kaback notes that " . . . the younger the child the greater the interest in the actual job performance itself. Most children are natural born actors; they want to act out in order to understand what it feels like to be a carpenter or a ball player."[13] The question is not — should attitudes toward work be taught in early elementary school? Students do, in fact, possess work attitudes. Generally, these are favorable. At issue, then, is how to preserve positive attitudes so they may be used as a foundation for more realistic attitudes and understandings.[14]

1.    Shows awareness of the social usefulness of work

    1.1   Surveys various types of community workers
    1.2   Selects an occupation of interest and conducts independent study
    1.3   For the occupation selected, reports on the social contributions of that worker
    1.4   For the occupation selected, discusses the consequences of that worker not performing his/her job

2.    Shows awareness of how individual needs are met through work

    2.1   Illustrates how work can meet basic human needs
    2.2   Illustrates how work can meet needs for self-expression
    2.3   Recognizes that others may enjoy doing work that he/she finds unpleasant
    2.4   Describes how he/she feels after successfully completing a difficult work task
    2.5   Recognizes that most types of work are sexless

3.    Adopts identity of worker

    3.1   Lists various types of work tasks performed regularly
    3.2   Explains how the role of student is similar to that of an employed worker
    3.3   Describes how work done in school can affect him/her in the future

## Accommodation Stage, Grades 4-6

During the Awareness Stage children are perceptually oriented; they make judgments in terms of how things look to them. In the period from about age nine to eleven, certain mental operations begin to manifest themselves, e.g., the ability to be aware of a previous thought. According to Almy, the intermediate years of education, which correspond approximately to Piaget's stage of concrete operations, are the time of intellectual development when the child is able to solve problems and give explanations in terms of concrete data.[15] The most important specific changes in cognitive development which take place with increasing age have been summarized by Vinacke as follows:

1.    Progression from single to complex concepts. For example, concepts of the structure of society move from the immediate family group to the neighborhood, school, community, and so on.

2.    Progression from diffuse to diffentiated concepts. Thus, concepts of the self change from generalized awareness of the body and relations to others, to well-organized knowledge of roles, attitudes, traits, etc., in a complex system of needs, social relationships, and activities.

3.  Progression from egocentric to more objective concepts. In the first or second grade, for example, a child may assume that a teacher knows much more about his home and parents. Later, of course, he learns to an increasing degree to treat objects and people as distinct from his own experience with them.

4.  Progression from concrete to abstract concepts. In this trend, the child tends to become increasingly free from the immediately perceived properties and functions of objects and to deal with them in the classificatory sense mentioned above. For example, a younger person tends to draw pictures of particular persons (himself or his mother), whereas older children can more readily produce a man or a child.

5.  Progression from variable to more stable concepts. In earlier school years the rules of a game or a classroom procedure are not treated as having a set form, whereas they come in due course to be regarded as fixed. Words which at first have no stable meaning are increasingly used to signify the same kind of object and characteristics of objects.

6.  Progression from inconsistent to more consistent and accurate concepts. A child in the first grade may consider any building with red clapboards to be an instance of a barn.[16]

These changes are continuous and cumulative and are not confined solely to the intermediate level of elementary school education. Certain kinds of concepts, such as those pertaining to self, undergo very extensive development in adolescence and, often, into young adulthood. The significant feature of these cognitive changes in the Accommodation phase of career development is that they occur more rapidly in childhood than in later years.

## Goals and Rationale

**B1.** *Developing greater self knowledge.* In this phase, children begin to conceptualize what they formerly only perceived.[17] "Self-concepts are self-percepts which have acquired meaning and which have been related to other self-percepts. A self-concept is the individual's picture of himself, the perceived self with accrued meanings."[18] Operationally, self-concept development at this level takes the form of helping students develop "self-understanding." Turner points out that the greater an individual's understanding of the activities in which he or she is interested, the ability to participate in those activities, and the value of those activities to the individual, the more accurate will be the choice of a later career.[19]

An additional operational aspect of self-understanding is the provision for periodic assessment of growth and learning, and the assimilation of new information. By becoming more fully aware of characteristics of the process of change which mark growth and development, children can: (a) begin to develop a better understanding of themselves at a certain point in time, i.e., a concept of becoming, and (b) recognize that their understanding of self is constantly changing, i.e., they are in a process of becoming.

1. Understands the terminology used for self-appraisal
   - 1.1 Reviews what is meant by interests
   - 1.2 Describes what is meant by aptitudes and abilities
   - 1.3 Describes what is meant by values
   - 1.4 Differentiates among interests, abilities, and values
2. Understands that interests may vary at different points in life
   - 2.1 Provides examples of how interests may change as a result of growth, learning, and new experience
   - 2.2 Explains the tendency of interests to become more stable as one grows older
3. Interprets how abilities influence choices and actions
   - 3.1 Differentiates between general ability and special ability
   - 3.2 Summarizes what is meant by the term ability
   - 3.3 Illustrates the role of abilities in relationship to interests
4. Interprets how values influence choices and actions
   - 4.1 Understands that values determine how an individual "feels" (importance, worth) toward an activity
   - 4.2 Differentiates own values toward various activities from those of peers
   - 4.3 Illustrates the role of values in relationship to interests
5. Formulates present self-identity reflecting knowledge of own abilities, interests, and values
   - 5.1 Summarizes primary areas of interest
   - 5.2 Compares present interests with those characteristic of earlier periods
   - 5.3 Provides examples of individual aptitudes and abilities
   - 5.4 Recognizes assets and limitations
   - 5.5 Provided with a list of activities, expresses the importance (value) of those activities to him/her
6. Judges the validity of own self-identity
   - 6.1 Recognizes that he/she has several identities
   - 6.2 Understands that the "me I see" may be different from the "me others see"
   - 6.3 Becomes aware of how others characterize him/her
   - 6.4 Compares own self-identity with the self others see

**B2.** *Developing concepts about the world of work.* At this level, the child moves from perceptualization of work activities and simple generalizations, such as goods and services workers, to more sophisticated concepts. If the child is to differentiate among thousands of occupations, he or she must be helped to develop a "cognitive map" which will serve as a conceptual framework for later occupational orientation and exploration. The emphasis should be on learning (a) what the world of work is and how it has evolved, (b) why occupations exist, (c) what is work, and (d) why people pursue various work activities (i.e., occupations).[20]

1.    Understands how people's basic needs are met through a culture

    1.1    Provides examples of basic human needs
    1.2    Describes how a culture develops to meet basic human needs
    1.3    Explains how a culture generates its own needs and requirements

2.    Understands that the world of work is composed of occupational establishments (factories, hospitals, stores) designed to meet cultural needs

    2.1    Explains why various occupational establishments have evolved
    2.2    Illustrates by example how a particular occupational establishment meets a specific cultural need
    2.3    Explains why industrialized cultures have a greater variety of occupational establishments
    2.4    Explains why industrialized cultures have a greater variety of service and leisure occupations

3.    Surveys various occupational establishments in relationship to three types of cultural needs

    3.1    Identifies those occupational establishments concerned with the *replenishment* of culture
    3.2.    Identifies those occupational establishments concerned with the *management and maintenance* of culture
    3.3    Identifies those occupational establishments concerned with the *transmission* of culture

**B3.** *Displaying increased responsibility for own behavior.* Awareness of individual responsibility for one's activities acquired in the previous stage now gives way to greater independence and a certain degree of authority to make decisions for oneself. Antholz states, "He has developed a sense of agency: He knows he can master parts of his environment."[21] The cultural desirability of extending a child's sense of agency has been emphasized by Havighurst: "... every society recognizes the growth of personal independence and initiative as desirable during middle childhood. The American society sets greater store than most by personal independence and starts training for independence at a relatively early age."[22]

1. Shows awareness that he or she is in charge of becoming a person

   1.1 Explains source of responsibility for own behavior
   1.2 Identifies ways to take responsibility for own behavior
   1.3 Identifies times in daily life for making own decisions
   1.4 Proposes why only the individual can develop own potentialities

2. Demonstrates awareness of individual responsibility for orderly development

   2.1 Recognizes that the future is built on the present
   2.2 Lists ways in which individual actions can affect progression toward a preferred goal
   2.3 Assumes personal responsibility for the consequences of his or her choices
   2.4 Relates the importance of education to planning one's own future

3. Demonstrates an awareness of the continuing process of change that characterizes maturation

   3.1 Describes a number of ways of "growing"
   3.2 Identifies commonalities in individual growth and development
   3.3 Differentiates own patterns of growth and development from others
   3.4 Recognizes that someday an occupational choice will have to be made
   3.5 Recognizes that life in the future will probably require continuing education and training
   3.6 Identifies the wide range of factors that influence growth and development

4. Engages in a wide range of occupationally related and leisure activities

   4.1 Participates in activities to test goals and aspirations
   4.2 Plans experiences in and out of school to capitalize on strengths and to strengthen weaknesses

**B4.** *Learning how to gather information and make decisions.* Learning how to meet change, adapt to it and to acquire the new skills demanded by occupational change, must begin early in the child's education. Students in grade six face at the end of the school year an important change — transfer to junior high school. Increasingly they are looking beyond their immediate world. The changes that are taking place become more significant in their conscious behavior. Therefore, it is important for children in the later elementary school years to develop behaviors and make decisions which will provide them with the greatest potential for occupational fulfillment under varied circumstances.

1.   Interprets why and how decisions are made

    1.1   Explains what is meant by a goal-directed decision
    1.2   Explains what is meant by a chance decision
    1.3   Identifies five recent decisions he/she has made
    1.4   For such decisions, differentiates between goal-directed and chance behaviors
    1.5   Discusses the results of goal-directed decisions
    1.6   Discusses the results of chance decisions

2.   Understands the nature of information-seeking skills

    2.1   Identifies three basic aspects of information-seeking: (a) asking appropriate questions, (b) determining completeness of information, and (c) determining accuracy of information
    2.2   Explains the difference between a restrictive question and a divergent question
    2.3   Illustrates the consequences of not having complete information
    2.4   Illustrates the consequences of not having accurate information

3.   Applies understanding of information-seeking skills to own career development

    3.1   Provides examples to illustrate relevant questions related to educational and occupational planning
    3.2   For such questions, decides the extent to which they are restrictive
    3.3   For such questions, states them in such a way as to provide complete information
    3.4   For such questions, states them in such a way as to provide accurate information
    3.5   Discusses the benefits of using information-seeking skills in decision-making

**B5.** *Showing awareness of the nature of group membership.* This goal relates very closely to B1 and is concerned with developing greater "social self" awareness. Self-understanding is nourished and enhanced by impressions or reflections of self received from others. Conversely, self-understanding contributes to the development of desirable social relationships. Turner maintains that the ability to communicate and cooperate with others is facilitated in proportion to the degree that individuals understand themselves.[23]

1.   Shows awareness of the importance of group skills

    1.1   Illustrates typical characteristics of family, play, and classroom groups
    1.2   Explains how group pressure can influence individual development both positively and negatively

      1.3   Identifies advantages of group problem solving
      1.4   Recognizes the need for group members to feel secure
      1.5   Recognizes that group cohesiveness requires effort to develop
      1.6   Recognizes that group skills must be learned experientially

2.    Demonstrates awareness of a "social self"

      2.1   Identifies ways he/she relates to other persons
      2.2   Attempts to characterize self as others see him/her
      2.3   Expands his/her capacity to understand the feelings of others
      2.4   Describes how a better understanding of self leads to better relations with others in group activities

3.    Shows awareness of the differences which exist between individuals and between groups

      3.1   Explains how "dislikes" develop, e.g., imitation, feelings of frustration
      3.2   Illustrates how people express dislikes about groups with which they are unfamiliar
      3.3   Describes how stereotypes develop
      3.4   Distinguishes between inherited and learned differences
      3.5   Differentiates among: prejudgment, prejudice, and stereotype

**B6**. *Accepting differences in work attitudes and value.* During the previous stage, the child manifests work attitudes and values by taking the role of various workers. As children become better able to conceptualize, their basis for choice becomes more rational. "Since living requires choosing between values, which are more or less desirable objects or modes of action, and since many important life situations require a choice between two or more values, the growing child must develop a scale of values which will enable him to make stable choices and to hold himself to these choices."[24] According to Antholz, if the value of work is not internalized, it becomes very difficult for the individual to achieve self-direction.[25] The probability that an individual will work only because and when others want him or her to work remains high. This, in turn, has a deleterious effect on the individual's ability to achieve the discipline of work or a positive self-concept. In this stage the child continues to develop his or her attitudes and values toward work, and in addition, develops a greater appreciation and acceptance of the attitudes and values of others.

1.    Shows awareness that individuals have different attitudes and values toward the same occupation

      1.1   Identifies work task which classmates share in common
      1.2   Describes why he/she likes or dislikes that task
      1.3   Compares own response to those of classmates
      1.4   Discusses why differences of opinion should be respected

2.    Shows awareness of the prevalence of different lifestyles and values

    2.1    Describes in own words what is meant by "life-style"
    2.2    Provides examples to illustrate different life-styles
    2.3    From among examples, identifies own preferred life-style
    2.4    Compares own life-style preference to those of classmates
    2.5    Discusses similarities and differences in life-style of persons having the same occupation
    2.6    Discusses why differences in life-styles should be respected

3.    Shows awareness of inequities related to the occupational roles of women

    3.1    Identifies occupations which are predominantly male
    3.2    Selects one male-dominated occupation and describes the work requirements of it
    3.3    Describes whether male dominance in the occupation studied is justified on the basis of work requirements
    3.4    Accepts or rejects the statement that women have been discriminated against in some occupations

### Orientation Stage: Grades 7 and 8

Career developmental tasks at the elementary school level have been little researched. Therefore, in the treatment of the previous two stages it was necessary to infer such behaviors from the writings of child development authorities such as Piaget, Erickson, and Havighurst. A much clearer picture of career development at the junior high school level, however, can be drawn. This situation is primarily the result of the work of Donald Super and his colleagues.

> Adolescence is seen as a period in which young people explore the world in which they live, the subculture of which they are about to become a part, the roles they may be expected to play, and the opportunities to play roles which suit their personalities, interests, and aptitudes. It is at the same time a period in which the adolescent through experience and self-examination *clarifies his self concept** and begins to put it into words, finds out what outlets exist in society for one who seeks to play a given role, and modifies his self concept to bring it in line with reality.[26]

> Vocational exploratory behavior refers to activities, mental or physical, undertaken with the more or less conscious purpose or hope of eliciting information about one's self or one's environment, or of verifying or arriving at a basis for a conclusion or *hypothesis which will aid in choosing,** preparing for, entering, adjusting to, or progressing in, an occupation.[27]

The author's decision to designate this stage of development as "orientation" rather than "exploration" follows from Jordaan's discussion of exploratory behavior. To be exploratory, an act should

---

* Emphasis added.

include aspects of (a) search, (b) experimentation, (c) investigation, (d) trial, and (e) hypothesis testing. "If these elements are not present, we propose that the term orientation be substituted for exploration. In other words, we would distinguish between becoming oriented to a situation and *exploring it.*"[28] While many of the tasks involved in achieving the goals of this stage do indeed involve exploration and would meet Jordaan's criteria, the more insightful and purposeful acts of trial and hypothesis testing are more characteristic of the next career development stage.

The crucial point in the orientation stage is at the end of junior high school, when the student is confronted with the necessity of making a curriculum decision prior to entering high school. The intimate relationship between education and career and the potential effects of this decision on later available options suggest that choice of a high school curriculum is, in a very real sense, as much a "career choice" as an educational one. As Katz[29] points out, when ". . . the adolescent is prompted by cultural expectations (especially the educational system) to think and act in terms of becoming, a becoming which will progressively be subjected to reality testing, then the occupational choice process has been put in motion. The eighth or ninth grade curriculum decision is the first of these formal choice-points. Like a stereoscope, it provides a means to bring perceptions of self and perception of alternatives for choice into the same field of vision, with one set of perceptions superimposed upon the other."

Behavioral changes in grades seven and eight are not nearly so much cognitive as they are affective and social. According to Piaget, early adolescents are in the stage of *formal operations* and can reason similarly to adults. They can examine the consequences of various combinations of factors in systematic and orderly fashion. They are able to devise theories, state them verbally, and then test them in actual practice.[30] Thus, according to Piaget's theory, most adolescents should be capable of dealing intellectually with the tasks which they confront during the exploration stage.

The more important problem of adolescence has been described by Erickson[31] and Ausubel[32] as that of establishing identity. In adolescence, the individual experiences a period of "developmental disequilibrium." At this time, adolescents must exchange "derived status" (i.e., role of parent satellite) for "primary status" (i.e., becoming persons in their own right). In this process, the formulation of a career objective plays a crucial role. "The chief agent in promoting these developments (shift in role) is exploration which furnishes the adolescent with opportunities to make choices and independent decisions, to play different kinds of adult roles, and to establish his own identity."[33]

**Goals and Rationale**

C1. *Clarifying occupational self-concept.* This goal relates to the process of organizing lower-order self-perceptions into newer, more comprehensive pictures of self. Super[34] points out that "... the concept of self is generally a picture of self in some role, some situation, in a position, performing some set of functions, or in some web of relationships." Formulation of a "career hypothesis," which is an expression of a career objective, based upon self data and information related to preferred occupations, is the end result of clarification. Behavior in this area is largely verbal. It becomes instrumental at the point when the career hypothesis is implemented via choice of high school curriculum.

1. Understands methods and procedures for self appraisal
    1.1 Describes the role of self appraisal in career planning and decision-making
    1.2 Illustrates the usefulness of self knowledge in career planning and decision-making
    1.3 Differentiates between formal and informal methods of self appraisal
    1.4 Identifies types of self information required for career planning

2. Demonstrates correct usage of self appraisal methods and procedures
    2.1 Completes representative self appraisal activities and/or inventories related to abilities, interests and values
    2.2 Explains relationships among abilities, interests and values
    2.3 Illustrates how knowledge of abilities, interests and values relates to career planning and decision-making

3. Formulates tentative career hypothesis
    (Note: The following objectives are based on use of *The Self Directed Search,* Form E[35] as a tool for aiding clarification of an occupational self-concept)
    3.1 Completes SDS assessment booklet
    3.2 Interprets meaning of SDS summary code
    3.3 Identifies ten occupations related to summary code
    3.4 Compares summary code occupations to "occupational daydreams"
    3.5 Given outcome of previous objective, prepares revised list of occupational preferences
    3.6 Collects information about occupational preferences
    3.7 Prepares tentative career plan for occupational and educational exploration

C2. *Surveying the structure and interrelatedness of the American economic system.* The desired outcomes for this goal involve discovery, new knowledge, and orientation to occupations, economics and technology. These behaviors and concepts are interrelated with the previous goal and are essential inputs to the formulation of a career hypothesis. An activity-oriented setting such as is found in the more progressive industrial arts laboratories is *one* of the more desirable "in-school" environments for (a) orientation to technological processes; (b) acquiring familiarity with occupational roles; and (c) developing vocabulary and understandings of the structure and organization of business, service and industrial enterprises.

1. Understands fundamental economic concepts

   1.1  Distinguishes among the three major components of economics: technology, resources, and institutions
   1.2  Explains what is meant by the "circular flow" of economic activity
   1.3  Summarizes the role that technology plays in economic change

2. Understands basic principles of the manpower market

   2.1  Explains the efforts that supply and demand have on the manpower market
   2.2  Summarizes changes that have taken place in the labor force since 1920
   2.3  Infers which industries and occupations will have the greatest employment potential in the future
   2.4  Discusses implications of labor market trends for own career planning

3. Relates the importance of education and training to American economic growth

   3.1  Explains what is meant by the phrase "education is a form of investment in human resources"
   3.2  Interprets the correlation between education and lifetime earnings
   3.3  Outlines the noneconomic benefits of education and training

4. Analyzes the institutional and occupational structure of the world of work

   4.1  Explains what is meant by an occupational cluster
   4.2  Distinguishes between occupational clusters and occupational classifications
   4.3  Illustrates ways in which occupations can be clustered
   4.4  Studies occupational clusters in terms of:
       (a)  purpose of each cluster
       (b)  types of enterprises and occupations within each cluster, and
       (c)  future demand for workers within each cluster

5.    Engages in simulation of various economic enterprises

    5.1.    Differentiates between two primary types of enterprises — goods and services

    5.2    Summarizes the five functions common to all economic enterprises: (a) managing, (b) research and development, (c) preparing to promote a service or produce a product, (d) providing services or producing products, and (e) selling services or products

    5.3    Establishes with classmates selected enterprises which perform five common functions

    5.4    Samples work activities representative of the enterprise

**C3.** *Recognizing responsibility for own career planning.* A sense of responsibility and initiative (i.e., sense of agency) in approaching the career planning tasks of this stage is the desired outcome of the present goal.[36] This behavior grows out of (a) recognition that career development is a longitudinal process requiring planning in earlier years and (b) understanding that planning helps to preserve freedom of choice and expands available options.

1.    Shows awareness of the need to begin career planning

    1.1    Discusses why it is necessary to begin early career planning

    1.2    Identifies the principal effects that a career has on an individual's life

    1.3    Justifies the importance of systematic career planning for a career

    1.4    Illustrates the consequences of not planning for a career

2.    Shows awareness that career development involves a succession of educational and occupational decisions

    2.1    Explains relationships between educational and occupational decisions

    2.2    Identifies present and future decision points

    2.3    Illustrates how one decision may affect subsequent ones

3.    Develops a projected high school program compatible with local educational requirements and tentative career hypothesis

    3.1    Identifies high school courses required of all students

    3.2    Explains how required course work may relate to tentative career hypothesis

    3.3    Identifies elective courses related to tentative career hypothesis

    3.4    Outlines extra-curricular and nonschool activities which can aid in progress toward career goals

**C4.** *Practicing information-seeking and decision-making methods.* Educational and occupational decision making during the latter part of the orientation stage relies upon the application of previously learned decision-making skills. Because career decision making is an individual act, the type and amount of personal, occupational, and educational data that each individual requires will vary. Therefore, students must be helped to learn (a) the *characteristics of data,* (b) *where* data may be obtained, (c) *how to use* information files and resources, and (d) *which* types of information best meets their needs at various stages of career development. Thus, curriculums for developing these skills have as their objectives "processes" of inquiry and decision making rather than more traditional subject matter or content oriented objectives.

1.  Understands what is involved in becoming a skillful decision-maker

    1.1  Defines what is meant by decision making, i.e., a process in which a person selects from two or more possible choices
    1.2  Distinguishes between problem solving and decision making
    1.3  Explains how a skillful decision-maker has more personal *freedom* and greater *control* over own life
    1.4  Identifies factors which tend to limit decisions, e.g., (a) by what a person is capable of doing, (b) by what a person is willing to do, and (c) by the environment
    1.5  Summarizes the three major requirements of skillful decision making: (a) examination and recognition of *values,* (b) knowledge and use of relevant *information,* and (c) knowledge and use of effective strategies
    1.6  Illustrates the range and type of decisions which individuals are required to make
    1.7  Differentiates between a "good" and a "poor" decision

2.  Understands the role of values in relation to decision making

    2.1  Contrasts the meanings of values and work values
    2.2  Identifies own work values through formal and/or informal means
    2.3  Illustrates the role of values in a given decision-making situation
    2.4  Applies knowledge of work values in educational decision making

3.  Understands the role of information seeking and evaluation skills in relation to the decision-making process

    3.1  Outlines the four steps involved in knowing the alternatives at a decision-point: (a) define the decision, (b) write down the existing alternatives, (c) list sources of help in discovering new alternatives, and (d) add new alternatives to those already identified
    3.2  Practices listing alternatives for given decision-points
    3.3  Illustrates that whether an alternative is acceptable or not is a matter of one's personal values
    3.4  Practices evaluating possible sources of information in making a decision

4.　Understands strategies for converting information into action

4.1　Illustrates how simple, daily decisions involve a degree of risk
4.2　Gives examples of the relation of emotions to risk taking
4.3　Rates self in relation to risk-taking tendencies
4.4　Differentiates among different types of risk-taking strategies
4.5　Practices application of risk-taking strategies

5.　Applies understanding of information-seeking skills to consideration of possible educational-occupational goals

5.1　Defines the decision including when it has to be made
5.2　Identifies existing alternatives he/she knows about
5.3　Lists sources of help in discovering new alternatives
5.4　Adds new alternatives to those previously identified

**C5.** *Participating in simulated, group work activities.* The importance of adolescent social development to later life adjustment has been underscored by Havighurst.[37] Of equal importance and related to later occupational adjustment is the need to provide students with opportunities to *learn to work together* as peers. Long ago, John Dewey argued that if children are to live democratically, they have to experience the living process of democracy in the classroom. The author maintains that the same can be said for cooperative work behavior.

1.　Shows awareness of how economic change effects the social nature of work

1.1　Explains why growth of service-oriented enterprises has resulted in greater need for workers with effective interpersonal skills
1.2　Provides examples of service-oriented enterprises which are highly social in nature
1.3　Explains why specialization and division of labor contributes to need for greater interpersonal skills

2.　Recognizes the social nature of an economic enterprise

2.1　Outlines a typical personnel organization structure
2.2　Identifies the level of responsibility associated with various work roles
2.3　Relates how workers at all levels contribute to the goal of an enterprise
2.4　Identifies the interpersonal skills associated with different levels of authority
2.5　Describes the interpersonal skills which make for individual success or failure within an organization

3. Practices interpersonal skills in simulated enterprises

    3.1 Displays ability to get along with "employer" and "co-workers"

    3.2 Contributes to achievement of group goals

    3.3 Relates to others through understanding and compassion

**C6.** *Appreciating the role of work in meeting social and individual needs.* Whereas goal C2 was concerned to a large degree with developing concepts about the economic nature and functions of work, this goal relates to developing attitudes and appreciations about the noneconomic aspects of work. For most people, work is no longer limited to only a means of making a living by the sweat of the brow. Work is, and can continue to be in the future, a source for meeting social and psychological needs. An important part of student's orientation to the world of work during this stage should be a consideration of how work can contribute to individual well-being in non-material ways.

1, Shows awareness of the non-economic nature and functions of work

    1.1 Differentiates between "work" and "labor"

    1.2 Identifies the economic functions of work in both societal and human terms, i.e., (a) to produce goods and services, and (b) as a means to earn a living

    1.3 Explains how work can contribute to individual development

    1.4 Provides examples to illustrate how work can meet personal and psychological needs

2. Shows awareness of the relation between work and human needs

    2.1 Distinguishes between a "need" and a "want"

    2.2 Identifies five common types of needs:
(a) physiological, (b) safety, (c) belongingness, (d) esteem, and (e) self-actualization

    2.3 Describes what is meant by a hierarchy of needs

    2.4 Illustrates how work may satisfy different levels of human needs

    2.5 Discusses the relation between job satisfaction and mental health

3. Shows awareness of the reciprocal relationship between individuals and their work

    3.1 Explains what is meant by the phrase: "You are what you do"

    3.2 Identifies ways in which a job affects a person's life style

    3.3 Reads case studies about people and their attitudes toward work

    3.4 Illustrates how one can define the nature and meaning of a job through his/her attitudes toward work

4.   Shows concern for the work values of the opposite sex
    4.1   Identifies multiple life roles of males and females
    4.2   Summarizes factors affecting changes in traditional male and
          female roles
    4.3   Defends the need for elimination of sexism in education and
          work
    4.4   Illustrates changes (individual and occupational) which have
          resulted from efforts to eliminate sexism in work

## Exploration and Preparation Stage: Grades 9-12

During the four years of high school the adolescent is expected
to *crystallize* an occupational choice and evidence commitment to
that goal by embarking upon a specialized education or training program or by taking an entry level job upon leaving school. Behaviors
in this stage differ from the previous ones in *degree* of intent and
purposefulness *rather than in kind or type.* At the end of the orientation stage, the typical student formulates a "career hypothesis." This
serves as a symbol for a number of preferred occupational activities
and life goals. Although this act is an important prerequisite to subsequent selection of more specific goals, two characteristics tend to
be lacking: *reality testing* and *commitment.* Whereas behavior in the
orientation stage is generally characterized by *search, experimentation,* and *investigation,* behavior in the exploration and preparation
stage deals more with *trial* and *hypothesis testing.* "By hypothesis
testing we mean behavior which is engaged in for the purpose of
checking the validity of some more or less clearly formulated belief,
hypothesis, or expectation concerning the self or the environment.[38]

The tasks at this stage, then, require the student to expand and
refine behaviors of earlier stages. "At this level, the concepts which
students hold about self, the work world, and career preparation
become internalized and form the basis for more specific generalizations concerning career life identity. Students at this level begin to
take on certain features of real occupational roles related to their
visualized career life."[39] Above all, it is important to acknowledge
that the stakes are considerably higher at the end of this period than
at the end of previous ones.

> Guidance at the eighth- (8 or 9) or ninth-grade choice-point could look
> ahead to student development under the continuing shelter of the second-
> ary school . . . change would generally involve some loss: [the student]
> learned that the rules of the decision-making game required him to play
> 'for keeps.' But the stakes were low . . . the institutional protection of the
> school and its guidance program provided him with a beginning climate for
> inexpensive exploration and try-out . . . Now, at grade 11 or 12, both
> thought and observation are presumed to be ready for more severe test.[40]

## Goals and Rationale

**D1**. *Crystallizing and implementing occupational self-concept.* The process of career development involves the formulation and reformulation of the self-concept throughout the life stages. Super *et al.*[41] have repeatedly pointed out differences in the level of complexity of the self-concept. For example, in the orientation stage, behavior was predominantly verbal as the individual clarified a career hypothesis. In the exploration and preparation stage the behavior becomes more instrumental as the self-concept is (a) tested and reformulated through occupational exploration and (b) implemented through commitment to a preferred occupation or educational option. Thus, as Super[42] points out, "The complex self-concept is organized within the framework of a role."

1.   Validates interests, abilities, and aptitudes through occupational exploration

    1.1   Engages in representative, sample work activities
    1.2   Discovers the level of responsibility associated with various work roles
    1.3   Completes task specifications for given work activities
    1.4   Conducts self evaluations of the products of own work
    1.5   Summarizes new interests, abilities, and aptitudes resulting from occupational exploration

2.   Reformulates career exploration-preparation plan (Note: Refer to Goal C1 for related objectives)

    2.1   Completes SDS booklet
    2.2   Interprets meaning of SDS summary codes
    2.3   Identifies a representative sample of occupations related to summary codes
    2.4   Relates summary code occupations to those of previously developed career exploration plan
    2.5   Modifies career plan as a result of exploratory experiences

3.   Judges the validity of own career plan

    3.1   Solicits assistance from counselor (and others) to help evaluate career plan
    3.2   Reviews cumulative record to help confirm areas of greatest strength
    3.3   Identifies weaknesses and limitations
    3.4   Completes diagnostic tests, interests inventories and/or other instruments for additional self data
    3.5   Develops plan for strengthening weaknesses
    3.6   Summarizes why he/she qualifies for intended career goals

**D2**. *Executing plans to qualify for post-secondary career objectives.* The relation of this goal to D1 above is obvious. The crystallization and implementation of the self-concept is a gradually evolving one, pieced together from bits of experience acquired during this stage (and beyond). The purpose of the present goal is for the student to *qualify* for preferred career objectives through appropriate study and occupational experience. In grades nine and ten the student will explore several occupational clusters to (a) test the career hypothesis formulated in the earlier stage, and (b) narrow the range of his or her occupational cluster preferences. An outcome of occupational exploration in grades nine and ten will be the selection of *one* occupational cluster for preparation in greater depth in grades eleven and twelve. The type of course work pursued in the last two years will of necessity depend on whether the student opts for (a) entry-level employment (b) post-high school technical education or (c) post-high school baccalaureate education.

1.  Understands relation of economic benefits to levels of education

    1.1  Identifies three ways an individual's economic future is affected by his/her level of education: (a) amount of income, (b) ability to compete, and (c) job stability

    1.2  Explains relationship between job competition and level of education completed

    1.3  Explains relationship between holding a job and level of education completed

    1.4  Compares potential lifetime earning power to level of education completed

    1.5  Interprets graphical relationships between unemployment and level of education completed

2.  Explores occupational clusters to validate occupational preferences and to develop new knowledge and skills

    2.1  Outlines types of economic enterprises representative of various occupational clusters

    2.2  Increases the range of occupations of which he/she has a knowledge

    2.3  Engages in work activities representative of preferred occupational cluster(s)

    2.4  Engages in part-time work, volunteer activities, and extra-curricular activities associated with preferred career goals

    2.5  Summarizes new knowledge and skills resulting from occupational exploration

    2.6  Shows awareness of the nature of small business ownership (i.e., entrepreneurship)

3.  Pursues supervised work experience (cooperative vocational education or experience-based career education)

    3.1  Applies previously developed basic academic skills to work tasks

    3.2   Applies previously developed occupational competencies to work tasks

    3.3   Assesses own progress periodically in developing greater occupational competency

    3.4   Identifies worker functions which require additional education or training

    3.5   Identifies educational opportunities offered by employer and/or unions to advance on the job

4.   Demonstrates understanding of job-seeking methods and skills

    4.1   Prepares personal data sheet (resume)

    4.2   Completes sample job application forms

    4.3   Prepares sample letters of application

    4.4   Participates in simulated employment interview

    4.5   Evaluates performance of self and others in relation to simulated employment interview

5.   Demonstrates information-seeking skills in relation to educational and occupational information

    5.1   Identifies resource tools to use in studying an occupation

    5.2   Formulates criteria for evaluating occupational information

    5.3   Collects information about the many available occupations within a preferred occupational family

    5.4   Analyzes preferred occupations to determine future employment outlook, worker functions, and job requirements

    5.5   Summarizes the educational requirements and the types and costs of education and training programs for which he/she has an interest

**D3.** *Displaying commitment to implementation of a career plan.* "Exploratory behavior may be systematic and planful or it may be random, haphazard, and diffuse."[43] An attitude essential to systematic career behavior is the individual's commitment to plan. Super[44] points out that the attitude, not the act, of commitment is a key factor in the specification of an occupational preference. The outcome at this level is what Morrill and Forrest have called an *active agent.* "The focus . . . is to provide the individual with the view of himself as having the 'power' to make a commitment and to influence and create his future."[45]

1.   Shows awareness of the need to possess basic academic skills and occupational competence

    1.1   Identifies reasons why many individuals drop out of school

    1.2   Explains why most employers prefer high school graduates

    1.3   Characterizes the career patterns of many high school dropouts: (a) last hired, (b) first fired, (c) lower pay, (d) poorer jobs

    1.4   Identifies ways in which high school dropouts may complete education
    1.5   Illustrates how automation is likely to change the number and type of available jobs

2.   Recognizes contingencies affecting implementation of a career plan

    2.1   Relates how personal compromises may have to be made in order to attain a chosen career goal
    2.2   Identifies personal, situational, and social factors which may affect entrance and advancement in a career
    2.3   Acknowledges that many careers require postponing immediate rewards for later long-range rewards
    2.4   Identifies types of knowledge and skills utilized in one occupation which may transfer to another
    2.5   Illustrates how different occupations vary in the degree of personal freedom to define one's role

3.   Displays new self perspectives and sense of agency

    3.1   Illustrates how individuals have control over their own educational and occupational behavior
    3.2   Proposes how each individual has a responsibility for "making it"
    3.3   Accepts own personal limitation
    3.4   Develops plan for strengthening own self-image

**D4.** *Demonstrating competency in decision-making skills and strategies.* In a way, all previous career education goals are concerned with decision making, for it is the knowledge, skills, and attitudes related to self and work which are utilized in choosing between educational-occupational alternatives. Thus, as Martin[46] states, "The goal at this level is to insure that the complex interrelationship of specific factors, including personal, social, economic, and educational, provides an appropriate and realistic motivational basis to enable the individual to apply concepts and knowledge regarding work-life selection in planning and decision-making and determining appropriate action to achieve intended adult work life goals."

1.   Understands the role of values in the process of decision making

    1.1   Explains what is meant by the phrase "Decision making is using what you know to get what you want"
    1.2   Provides examples to illustrate what he/she wants out of life
    1.3   Discusses the extent to which he/she has the freedom to make decisions
    1.4   Illustrates how values are examples of learned behavior
    1.5   Explains why people have difficulty making decisions when they are unaware about their values
    1.6   Engages in value clarification exercises
    1.7   Practices skill of establishing objectives based on values

2.   Applies understanding of decision-making skills in relation to collecting information and evaluating information

   2.1   Summarizes four mistakes commonly made in collecting information: (a) not knowing alternatives, (b) not knowing possible outcomes, (c) misrepresenting importance of data, and (d) collecting useless information or irrelevant data

   2.2   Illustrates types of available information sources associated with various kinds of decisions

   2.3   Defends the need for objectivity in evaluating information for decision making

   2.4   Provides examples to illustrate that people "see" an object, event, data, etc. differently

   2.5   Identifies information sources which are assumed to be without bias

   2.6   Illustrates the role of experience (one's own and other's) as a basis of information in deciding

3.   Applies understanding of decision-making skills in relation to risk taking and predicting possible outcomes

   3.1   Explains what is meant by the term "risk" (i.e., possibility of several outcomes)

   3.2   Summarizes factors associated with risk taking: (a) importance of the outcome, (b) present condition of risk-taker, (c) amount of information available, and (d) personality traits

   3.3   Relates the role of risk taking to decision making

   3.4   Practices skills in relation to predicting possible outcomes associated with various sample situations (e.g., dropping out of school, getting married, joining the military service, going to college)

4.   Demonstrates correct usage of decision-making skills and strategies

   4.1   Summarizes four different types of decision-making strategies: (a) wish strategy, (b) safe strategy, (c) escape strategy, and (d) combination strategy.

   4.2   Illustrates how every decision involves a strategy (reason), even though it may not be explicit

   4.3   Practices decision-making skills and strategies in relation to case studies and simulation exercises

**D5.** *Demonstrating effective interpersonal skills in relation to work.* Opportunities for students to work together in group situations, which was the focus for goal C5, should be continued at this level. Students should develop expanded awareness of the factors that facilitate or inhibit group functioning. Reports from employers repeatedly underscore the fact that failure of an empoloyee is due more often to lack of cooperative work relationships than to actual job skill performance. Peters and Farwell[47] describe many different roles that are indicative of various levels of operation within a functional group. These are examples of types of roles with which students should become acquainted. Group experiences should help students discover how each individual can contribute to or detract from satisfaction of group needs and goals.

1. Shows awareness of how one member's actions may affect the whole group

   1.1 Describes how the performance of any member of a work group can affect the group's performance

   1.2 Identifies the effects of a member's actions on other workers and describes the member's responsibilities to them because of these effects

2. Recognizes the social roles and demands required for successful performance in a work situation

   2.1 Describes human relations skills that are useful in a work setting

   2.2 Demonstrates sensitivity to the needs of employers and co-workers

   2.3 Understands the extent to which command of the fundamental processes of communication is necessary in a group-oriented work setting

3. Demonstrates ability to both compromise and exercise influence in the achievement of group goals

   3.1 Lists group goals in a given situation and identifies reasons why one may have to compromise to reach those goals

   3.2 Describes how one's influence might help to achieve group goals

   3.3 Identifies advantages and disadvantages of compromise and influence in a given situation

   3.4 Identifies ways in which one is dependent upon the work of others

   3.5 Identifies ways in which others depend upon work a person does

**D6**. *Demonstrating effective work habits and attitudes.* Preparation for employment is often only regarded as the mastery of job skills and related knowledge. The concern of goal D2 is, in part, for the individual to acquire skills to qualify for one of three career paths. The type of skills to be developed varies in relation to the chosen career objective. The present goal, however, is considered to be important for *all* students to acquire in order to be able to function effectively with various life demands. The individual who has internalized a value to work displays a drive to act out that behavior. He/she approaches work and other tasks in a systematic manner, completes tasks at or beyond the level of proficiency required, and derives satisfaction from the products of his or her efforts.

1.  Shows awareness of employee and employer responsibilities and obligations

    1.1  Identifies responsibilities and obligations that both employee and employer have a right to expect
    1.2  Defends the work role expectations of an employer
    1.3  Outlines types of factors which relate to success in a job
    1.4  Justifies the need for work rules and regulations

2.  Displays effective work habits

    2.1  Listens or reads attentively to prescribed instructions
    2.2  Pursues prescribed tasks in organized, methodical manner
    2.3  Adheres to prescribed standards for workmanship and performance
    2.4  Demonstrates proper use and care of tools and machines
    2.5  Displays appropriate safety consciousness
    2.6  Completes assigned work on time
    2.7  Evaluates products of own efforts

3.  Displays effective work attitudes

    3.1  Discusses what is meant by the following in relation to the role of an employee: (a) cooperation, (b) honesty, (c) initiative, (d) willingness to learn, (e) willingness to follow directions, (f) enthusiasm, (g) acceptance of criticism, and (h) loyalty
    3.2  Judges the validity of each of the above as a measure of employment success
    3.3  Appraises self and others in relation to work attitudes
    3.4  Develops self-improvement plan in relation to work attitudes

4.  Demonstrates understanding and appreciation of the role of work in one's life

    4.1  Reads case studies in which "successful" men and women reflect on the meaning of work in their own lives
    4.2  Interprets the meaning of the following phrases:
         (a)  "The harder I work the luckier I get"
         (b)  "Ideas don't work unless we do"
         (c)  "By the work one knows the workman"
    4.3  Identifies instances in which work has provided personal satisfaction and fulfillment
    4.4  Participates in class discussion about the various meanings associated with work
    4.5  Formulates own personal definition of work

## Summary

This chapter has presented a career education curriculum model augmented and refined from one developed earlier by Bailey and

128 Career Education for Teachers and Counselors

Stadt.[48] The model seeks to facilitate the acquisition of career development concepts, attitudes and skills as the primary learning outcomes of career education. The importance of focusing on career development is made obvious by Super, who states: "When the concepts of career development are more widely understood, and when its methods and materials are more visible, career education will have come of age."[49]

REFERENCES

1. Hoyt, K.B. *An Introduction to Career Education: A Policy Paper of the U.S. Office of Education.* Washington, D.C.: U.S. Government Printing Office, 1975, p. 4.

2. Vinacke, W.E., "Concept Formation in Children of School Ages," in A.R. Binter and S.H. Frey, eds., *The Psychology of the Elementary School Child.* Chicago: Rand McNally, 1972. pp. 135-145.

3. Ibid.

4. Formanek, R. and Morine, G., "Categorizing in Young Children: Two Views," in Binter and Frey, eds., *The Psychology of the Elementary School Child,* pp. 145-158.

5. Vinacke, pp. 135-145.

6. Super, D.E., *Career Development: Self-Concept Theory.* New York: College Entrance Examination Board, 1963.

7. Goodson, S., "Children Talk About Work." *Personnel and Guidance Journal,* 49 (1970), 131-136.

8. Zimmerman, B., and Bailey, L.J., *Children's Conceptions About Work and Play,* Career Development for Children Project. Carbondale, Southern Illinois University, February, 1971.

9. Formanek and Morine, p. 154.

10. Hill, G.E. and Luckey, F.B., *Guidance for Children in Elementary Schools.* New York: Appleton-Century-Crofts, 1969, p. 14.

11. Havighurst, R.J. *Human Development and Education.* New York: David McKay, 1953, p. 31.

12. Hill and Luckey, p. 16.

13. Kaback, G.R., "Occupational Information for Groups of Elementary School Children." *Vocational Guidance Quarterly,* 14 (1969), 167.

14. Herr, E.L., *Decision-Making and Vocational Development.* Boston: Houghton Mifflin, 1970.

15. Almy, M., "Wishful Thinking About Children's Thinking?" *Teacher's College Record,* 62 (1961), 396-406.

16. Vinacke, pp. 142-143.

17. Antholz, M.B., "Conceptualization of a Model Career Development Program, K-12." Unpublished research paper, University of Minnesota, 1972.

18. Super, p. 18.

19. Turner, K.G., *A Conceptual Model of the Functional Self.* Career Development for Children Project. Carbondale, Illinois: Southern Illinois University, 1972.

20. Van Rooy, W.H. and Bailey, L.J., *A Conceptual Model of the World of Work,* Career Development for Children Project. Carbondale, Illinois: Southern Illinois University, 1972.

21. Antholz, p. 30.

22. Havighurst, p. 39.

23. Turner, Op. cit.

24. Havighurst, p. 36.

25. Antholz, Op. cit.

26. Jordaan, J.P., "Exploratory Behavior: The Formation of Self and Occupational Concepts," in D.E. Super, et al., *Career Development: Self-Concept Theory.* New York: College Entrance Examination Board, 1963, p. 51.

27. Jordaan, p. 59.

28. Jordaan, p. 56.

29. Katz, M., *Decisions and Values: A Rationale for Secondary School Guidance.* New York: College Entrance Examination Board, 1963, p. 33.

30. Almy, Op. cit.

31. Erickson, E., *Identity: Youth and Crisis.* New York: Norton, 1968.

32. Ausubel, D.P., *Theory and Problems of Adolescent Development.* New York: Grune and Stratton, 1954.

33. Jordaan, p. 47.

34. Super, p. 18.

35. Holland, J.L., *The Self Directed Search: Form E.* Palo Alto, California: Consulting Psychologists Press, 1973.

36. Tiedeman, D.V., "The Agony of Choice: Guidance for Career Decisions," in R.C. Pucinksi and S.P. Hirsch, eds., *The Courage to Change: New Directions for Career Education.* Englewood Cliffs, New Jersey: Prentice-Hall, 1971. pp. 121-130.

37. Havighurst, Op. cit.

38. Jordaan, p. 56.

39. Gysbers, N.C. and Moore, E.J., "Career Development in The Schools," in G.F. Law, ed., *Contemporary Concepts in Vocational Education.* Washington, D.C.: American Vocational Association, 1971. p. 226.

40. Katz, p. 42

41. Super, Op. cit.

42 Super, p. 18.

43. Jordaan, p. 65.

44. Super, Op. cit.

45. Morrill, W.H. and Forrest, D.J., "Dimension of Counseling for Career Development," *Personnel and Guidance Journal,* 49 (1970), p. 303.

46. Martin, A.M., *The Theory and Practice of Communicating Educational and Vocational Information.* Boston: Houghton Mifflin, 1971. pp. 30-31.

47. Peters, H.J. and Farwell, G.G., *Guidance: A Developmental Approach.* Chicago: Rand McNally, 1967, pp. 275-276.

48. Bailey and Stadt, Op. cit.

49. Super, D.F.. *Career Education and the Meanings of Work.* Washington, D.C.: U.S. Government Printing Office, 1976, p. 42.

# 5

## PLANNING, IMPLEMENTING and EVALUATING CAREER EDUCATION

---

### Introduction

In Chapter Four the *ends* (or learning outcomes) of career education were introduced and elaborated. In this chapter, the *means* will be discussed and a representative lesson planning process will be illustrated for how to brings ends and means together. The focus of the chapter is on demonstrating how career education can be implemented with relative ease using established educational principles and methods and employing available instructional materials and evaluation tools.

### Principles of Curriculum Planning

Curriculum development principles and processes have been discussed in a text chapter by Bailey.[1] Based on his 14 principles of curriculum development for career education, five principles of *curriculum planning* can be extracted. The phrase "curriculum planning" is used rather than "curriculum development" because the role of the teacher is that of planning and implementing curriculum rather than developing curriculum. The principles are:

1. A curriculum model should be employed which clearly states the basic purpose of the curriculum in terms of its long-range learner effects.

2. The curriculum should have stated goals and objectives in terms of desired learning outcomes.

3. The structure and organization of learning outcomes should take into account the developmental capabilities, interests and limitations of students at various age-grade levels.

131

4.  The instructional content of the curriculum should consist of a wide array of topics, activities, and materials which are intentionally selected to facilitate the desired learning outcomes.

5.  The preparation of learning units and lessons should be based upon tested theories and principles of teaching and learning.

The curriculum model contained in the previous chapter seems to meet Principles 1, 2, and 3. The remaining part of this chapter will illustrate how Principles 4 and 5 can be accomplished.

## Identifying Instructional Content and Methods

Once objectives are stated, the teacher or counselor either develops or selects appropriate instructional methods and materials. In actual practice, both approaches are used. It is recommended that teachers and counselors become familiar with existing resources and materials before beginning to develop their own. Since 1970, thousands of materials, both commercial and noncommercial, have been produced. A number of surveys have been conducted, as follows, to catalog and evaluate these materials:

1.  *Search and Assessment of Commercial Career Education Materials.* Peat, Marwick, Mitchell and Co., 1972. (ED 075 657)

2.  *Instructional Materials for Career Education: A Search and Assessment for the Office of Education.* Peat, Marwick, Mitchell and Co., 1974. (ED 090 441)

3.  *Abstracts of Instructional Materials for Career Education.* Bibliography Series No. 15, The Center for Vocational and Technical Education, 1972. (ED 068 627)

4.  *Supplement to Abstracts of Instructional Materials for Career Education.* Bibliography Series No. 16, The Center for Vocational and Technical Education, 1973. (ED 975 576)

5.  *Review and Analysis of Sources of Occupational Information for Career Education.* Information Series No. 89, The Center for Vocational and Technical Education, 1973. (ED 079 482)

6.  *EPIE Career Education Selection and Evaluation Tools: Volume 2, Analyses of Seven Hundred Prescreened Materials.* EPIE Institute, 1975.

7.  "The Status of Career Education as Reflected in Instructional and Reference Materials." In D. H. McLaughlin, *Career Education in the Public Schools 1974-75: A National Survey.* American Institutes for Research, May 1976. (ED 122 165)

8.  "A Taxonomy of Commercial Instructional Materials for Career Education." In L. J. Bailey (Ed.), *A Teacher's Handbook on Career Development for Students With Special Needs: Grades K-12.* Illinois Office of Education, 1977. (ED 144 319)

These resources are valuable in helping practitioners to identify potential materials by title and publisher. Because new materials are continually being produced, it is recommended that you contact publishers and request them to place your name on their mailing list to receive annual career education materials catalogs. Names and addresses of publishers can be obtained from the above references.

The career education coordinator in each state department of education can be contacted for assistance in locating materials. Many states have instructional materials libraries which can loan materials. The state career education coordinator can also provide information about the availability of state and federal funds for use in purchasing instructional materials.

The implementation of career education is not limited only to self-contained classrooms and the use of printed and audiovisual materials. Indeed, many learning outcomes for career education require simulated and experiential learning, often in non-school settings. Considerable effort has been spent by career educators in enlisting support from parents and community groups in the implementation of career education. Refer back to the listings of publications at the end of Chapter Two for titles dealing with parental and community involvement in the implementation of career education.

Another approach to becoming familiar with career education implementation methods is to review descriptions of past demonstration projects that have been conducted with the aid of state and federal funds. The Office of Career Education of the U.S. Office of Education has published profiles of career education projects supported under the 1974 legislation. Following are compilations of project descriptions funded during fiscal years 1975 through 1978 (the four years during which the legislation was in operation):

*Profiles of Career Education Projects: First Year's Program; Fiscal Year 1975 Funding.* Prepared for the Office of Career Education, U.S. Office of Education, by Ohio State University, Columbus, Ohio, December 1975, 255 pp. (ED 120 411).

*Profiles of Career Education Projects: Second Year's Program; Fiscal Year 1976 Funding.* Prepared for the Office of Career Education, U.S. Office of Education, by Pacific Consultants, Washington, D.C., December 1976, 224 pp. (ED 138 786).

*Profiles of Career Education Projects: Third Year's Program; Fiscal Year 1977 Funding.* Prepared for the Office of Career Education, U.S. Office of Education, by Thomas Buffington and Associates, Washington, D.C., April 1978, 290 pp. (ED 158 005).

*Profiles of Career Education Projects: Fourth Year's Program; Fiscal Year 1978 Funding.* Prepared for the Office of Career Education, U.S. Office of Education, by Thomas Buffington and Associates, Washington, D.C., February 1979, 278 pp. (ED 167 775).

Two other resources published by the Office of Career Education contain descriptions of successful projects and activities. They are entitled *It's Working . . . Collaboration in Career Education*[2] and *Career Education Programs That Work.*[3] The latter publication describes nine projects that have been certified by the Joint Dissemination Review Panel (JDRP). All JDRP approved projects are subject to rigorous screening before they are cited as projects of proven effectiveness. Articles by High[4] and Kaplan and Hamilton[5] elaborate the nature of the JDRP review process.

### Lesson Planning for Career Education

We are now ready to consider how ends and means can be brought together to facilitate career development. The vehicle is the lesson plan. Untold numbers of lesson plan formats have been developed by teachers and teacher educators. There is no single right way for developing a lesson plan. The one used here represents an eclectic approach that has evolved during ten years of working with preservice and inservice teachers. The major criteria to be met by any lesson plan are: (a) it should be comprehensive enough to provide all information necessary to instruct the lesson, (b) it should be simple enough so as not to consume an inordinate amount of development time, and (c) it should lead to successful achievement of the stated objectives.

A two-part blank lesson plan form is displayed in Appendix A-1. Several completed sample lesson plans are also contained in Appendix A. Study the two-part form and completed examples briefly before continuing.

### Lesson Plan: Part I

According to Krathwohl[6] and Cole,[7] curriculum planning involves the process of moving through descending abstractions from very general and global statements of desired program behaviors to intermediate-level statements which indicate the building blocks from which the program will be constructed. Several levels of description are necessary to judicious planning of education processes. It is very important that a curriculum have a network of logically related objectives. The three levels of generality recommended by Krathwohl and Cole are shown in Figure 5:1. A discussion of these levels follows:

> **A.** At the first and most abstract level are the general statements most useful in the development of programs of instruction or the laying out of types of courses and areas to be covered. These are goals toward which several years of education might be aimed. There should be relatively few of these objectives. Their purpose is primarily to inform and influence.

Figure 5:1
RELATIONSHIPS AMONG THREE LEVELS OF CAREER DEVELOPMENT OBJECTIVES

| Generality | Application | Example |
|---|---|---|
| **Goals** — to inform and influence | Development of **programs** of instruction for several years of education (e.g., K-3, 4-6) | A1. Becoming aware of self characteristics |
| **General objectives** — defining areas of competency | Becomes the basis for instructional **units** | 1. Forms generalizations about self |
| **Specific objectives** — large in number and quite performance- and situation-specific | For creating **lessons** and instructional materials | 1.4 Recognizes uniqueness of own self |

They should reflect and be consistent with statements which describe the program's values and asusmptions about basic theoretical issues.

**B.** The second and more concrete level helps to analyze broad goals into more specific ones which are useful as the building blocks for instructional units. The second type of objectives should be greater in number and specificity. They should define areas of competence, perhaps as clusters of process skills which are quite performance-specific but situation-generalizable.

**C.** Third, there is a level needed to create instructional materials. These types of objectives should be large in number and quite highly performance- and somewhat more situation-specific. They should be viewed as a sample of a given number of possible objectives within a universe of acts or performances which might reasonably be inferred to foster the intermediate and global objectives.

Also shown in Figure 5:1, in the third column, is an example of how one curriculum goal for career education could be evolved into general and specific level objectives. The specific level objective is the one with which the practitioner is primarily concerned. We will now proceed to show how specific level objectives can be facilitated through the selection of appropriate instructional materials and through the implementation of a systematic, four-step process of instruction.

For illustrative purposes, refer to Appendix A-2. Note that the sample lesson plan provided is related to the broad Goal A1: "Becoming aware of self characteristics." This goal is suitable for students in grades K through 3. One of the general objectives for the goal is that the student "Forms generalizations about self." This objective constitutes a broad class of knowledges and competencies. That is, there are many ways by which one can "Form(s) generalizations about self." This general objective is suitable for a comprehensive instructional unit composed of several more specific objectives and lessons. One of the specific objectives related to this general objective is that of "Recognizes uniqueness of own self." This specific objective is developed by the materials and activities contained in the lesson plan illustrated in Appendix A-2.

To begin lesson plan preparation, write the specific objectives to be developed on the page under "Specific Objective(s)." Keep in mind that the number of specific objectives that can be stated is infinite. The actual number of objectives to be developed in one lesson plan will be dependent on the maturation and grade level of the particular students being instructed. Also keep in mind that the objectives contained in Chapter Four are only a representative, and not exhaustive, list. Additions, deletions, or modifications of the objectives may be made to meet the needs and psychological characteristics of the students present.

After the objectives to be developed have been stated on the lesson plan, the next step is to select (or develop) the instructional materials to be utilized. By way of example, the lesson plan in Appendix A-2 utilizes a commercial filmstrip and workbook. These two types of materials provide the basis for the activities in the lesson and are supplemented by teacher-developed activities. A point to be made related to the selection and development of learning materials and activities is that *multiple* learning activities and contexts should be used in instruction. This characteristic of lesson planning helps to assure that students master the objective and can apply the knowledge or skill in a future learning situation.

The last section of Part I deals with unique learner needs or characteristics. It is here that considerations are recorded about individuals or groups that need to be reflected in the course of instruction. Remember that the goal of education is to meet the needs of all learners, not just the majority.

### Lesson Plan: Part II

Once the objectives for a lesson plan have been identified, the materials to be used have been selected, and special learner needs noted, the methodology for conducting the lesson can be outlined. The second part of the blank lesson plan illustrated in Appendix A-1 will be used for this purpose. Even though lesson plan development may appear to be complex and time consuming, the teacher should appreciate that the long-term advantages outweigh the disadvantages. The facilitation of career development concepts and skills is too important to be left to chance. Lesson plan development helps to assure that the objectives of instruction are being met.

The approach used here is a simple and direct analysis of the teaching act. It may serve as a model of teaching for kindergarten, secondary school, university level, or elsewhere. The following discussion is relevant to all kinds of teaching. For purposes of illustration, however, it deals with teacher-directed instruction.

The four steps of the teaching process are: *Preparation, Presentation, Application,* and *Evaluation.* This four-step outline of the teaching process was originated in Germany by Herbart in the early 1800s. Over the years, the idea that teaching is essentially preparation, presentation, application, and evaluation has been alternately praised and condemned. Today, many prominent younger educational psychologists are again emphasizing the validity of this description of the teaching act. Although it has suffered some severe criticisms, this four-step analysis is once again finding wider acceptance. It may appear as three to six steps, and the steps may be characterized as differently (such as "systems approach"), but the underlying idea remains the same.

*Preparation Step.* Preparation here refers to *preparing the learner* to receive the instruction. A basic principle of learning is that students must have a need (i.e., readiness) for acquiring the specific information or skill to be taught. Students may already possess readiness or they may need to be motivated. The preparation step may be accomplished by one or more of the following:

1.    Students should be provided with an explanation of why the information or skill is important for them to learn. Avoid phrases such as, "Today we are going to talk about . . . ." Rather, introduce lessons along the line of, "Someday each of you will need to choose what type of career you are going to pursue. One way to help prepare to make that decision is to learn . . . ." The latter type of approach will help students to understand the significance of the lesson to be taught.

2.    In order for learning to take place, students must be both psychologically and physically at ease. The previous example is of the type designed to motivate students and to put them more at ease psychologically. With respect to providing the students' physical needs, suffice it to say that the teacher should do whatever is necessary by way of making the environment and surroundings conducive to learning.

3.    Another technique to prepare the learner is to teach from the known to the unknown. For example, a new lesson (unknown) should begin with the teacher explaining how previously learned material (known) relates to the new lesson. In this way students are helped to continue development of the knowledge and skill base already acquired.

*Presentation Step.* In this step the major learning strategy for the lesson is employed, be it by demonstration, film, group discussion, simulation, or other technique. The learning content should relate specifically to the performance objective which is stated as the outcome for the lesson. That is, if the objective is concerned with having students "identify their physical characteristics," then the presentation step should introduce and develop this concept.

Whereas the preparation step is based on the learning "principle of readiness," the presentation step is based on the learning "principle of effect." The principle of effect means that students have a need to be successful. Proper and effective presentation helps the learner to experience success. Further, success needs to be rewarded. Following are techniques which should be used to assure that students successfully learn the concept or skill being taught:

1.    Involve as many of the senses as possible. This is obviously crucial when dealing with students who have impairments of one or more senses.

2.    Proceed from simple to complex. Proceed in a logical, systematic fashion, e.g., tell - show - demonstrate - illustrate - question.

3.    Instruct slowly, clearly, and patiently. Students take five to ten times as long to acquire a concept or skill as an experienced person.

4.   Pause at intervals and ask questions to determine whether students are developing the desired outcome. Remember, telling is not synonymous with learning.

5.   Always recapitulate. At the end of the presentation, review and summarize the significant procedures and concepts in the lesson.

*Application Step.* After students have been prepared to receive the instruction and have been presented the concept or skill, opportunities to apply what has been learned must be provided. Research conducted on retention reveals that up to 80 percent of what has been learned one day is forgotten by the second day! This is not a casual observation. Rather, research on retention has been repeated over and over with the same consistent conclusion that forgetting takes place very rapidly at first and then slower and slower as time passes. To help students master and retain the desired concept or skill, the following techniques should be employed:

1.   Practice in applying the concept or skill should begin as soon as possible after instruction. In actual practice, the presentation and application steps should probably be combined. That is, let the learner do as much as possible while the lesson is being presented.

2.   Consider having students do as much of the teaching as possible. Again, research has shown that students who teach other students learn as much as or more than when they are taught by a teacher.

3.   Systematically space application over several days. Continual review and applications helps to prolong retention.

4.   Provide opportunities to apply the concept or skill in new situations. For example, the skill of decision-making should be applied in many different and varied circumstances, including decisions about what one does in his or her leisure time, how one spends money, how one may resolve a personal conflict, what occupation one might pursue in the future, and the like.

5.   The meaningfulness of material promotes retention. The preparation and presentation steps should have made apparent the meaningfulness of the concept or skill to be learned. In application, the learning activity should be concretely related to students' interests and needs. For example, the concept of "consumer" and "producer" can be made meaningful by illustrating how each person consumes and produces goods and services.

6.   Application should be as nearly individualized as possible. Students will learn at many different rates and with different degrees of effectiveness. The goal of instruction is for every student to master the desired learning outcome. Instruction of the next lesson should not proceed until each student has successfully learned the present one.

*Evaluation Step.* The last step in the systematic development of instruction is labeled evaluation, but would be more accurately characterized as "evaluation - feedback - correction." The purpose of this step, referred to as *formative* evaluation, is to assess the extent to which students are progressing toward completion of the lesson objectives. (The other type of evaluation which is done at the end of a course or term to assign grades is called *summative* evaluation.) The general procedures to be used during this step are as follows:

1. Begin to develop test items or test tasks by referring to the lesson objectives. For example, action verbs such as "identifies," "describes," "distinguishes," "computes," "draws," tell you what the student should be able to do.

2. Construct test items which measure each of the lesson objectives. Since the number of objectives will be small, it is a good idea to develop several items, both in number and type, for each objective. One useful technique is to reserve several learning activities for use as test tasks. For example, a workbook exercise can be used to *evaluate* learning in addition to *presenting* a lesson or *applying* a concept or skill.

3. For each item, decide on the criterion level of performance. Accuracy levels of 80 to 85 percent on each formative test are recommended as an indication of mastery.

4. Provide students with knowledge of results. For those students who have thoroughly mastered the lesson, the evaluation exercise should reinforce the learning and assure the student that his or her present mode of learning and approach to study is adequate.

5. For students who lack mastery, the test will reveal those objectives which need further work. This generally means that an additional amount of time may be all that is required.

6. Individual tutoring, self-study, peer teaching, and small group discussion sessions are among the techniques that can be successfully used with those students who need additional remedial work.

## Summary

The lesson planning process explained above and illustrated in Appendix A is not unique to career education. Rather, the recommended procedures are ones that have been employed by successful teachers for many years regardless of subject matter affiliation or grade level. Following is a step-by-step summary of procedures.

1. Prepare and duplicate multiple copies of the blank lesson plan form which is provided in Appendix A-1.

2. Review the nature of career development (Chapter Four) for the stage appropriate to the grade level of students being taught.

3. Given the appropriate stage, decide on which of the six goals you are going to address.

4.   Select the general level learning outcome to be developed. This objective, in effect, becomes a *unit theme* for which several lesson plans will be developed.

5.   Analyze the specific level objectives related to this general level objective. Decide how many lesson plans you will need to prepare in developing the general objective. You may have one or more objectives per lesson plan depending on the maturational level of the students involved.

6.   State the specific level objective(s) to be achieved. Remember that the objectives provided in Chapter Four are only samples of a nearly infinite number of possible outcomes. Adapt the wording of the objectives to accomodate any unique needs of the learners.

7.   *Stop.* Review Figure 5:1. Do you have clearly in mind the relationship among goals — general objectives — specific objectives?

8.   Now that the objectives for the lesson have been identified, select the topics, activities, and materials which will facilitate the objectives.

9.   Note any unique learner characteristics or needs that need to be accommodated.

10.  *Preparation step.* Select an activity that will motivate students and/or develop readiness.

11.  *Presentation step.* Select a major, important activity which is specifically designed to develop the lesson objective(s). This activity should be the most important one in the whole lesson. It should stimulate as many of the senses as possible.

12.  *Application step.* Students should be involved in doing something during this step. Multiple activities and contexts should be utilized to assure that all students successfully achieve the objective.

13.  *Evaluation step.* Feedback instruments or activities known as formative tests are administered to determine the extent to which students have learned the lesson objective(s). Individualized, remedial instruction is prescribed for those students who fail to achieve the specified level of performance.

14.  Review the lesson plan and rewrite or type in an easily readable form. A properly developed lesson is one capable of being used by another person without additional assistance.

    a.   Are the objectives logically related and properly stated?

    b.   Have all required materials, supplies, and equipment been listed?

    c.   Have any special learner needs and characteristics been provided for?

d.   Has the approximate time per activity been estimated? This will be useful for initial use, and should be revised after use, based on actual observed times.

e.   Are all four instructional steps sufficiently detailed so that another person could follow them? Are the steps logical and sequential?

15.   Repeat the above procedures for remaining lesson plans. Once completed, you should have a strong unit which develops the concept or skill stated by the general objective.

## Lessons and Units

With the exception of Figure 5:1, little reference has been made in this chapter to *instructional units*. The emphasis thus far has been on lesson planning, because an individual lesson is the basic element from which units are organized. Unit development is not a task separate from lesson development. Rather, a unit consists of nothing more than the collective individual lesson plans which have been developed to achieve the specific level objectives.

The relationship between lessons and unit is illustrated by the samples contained in Appendix A-4. Five, separate lesson plans have been developed as follows:

#1.   SDS Assessment (Objective 3.1)

#2.   The Meaning of Summary Codes (Objectives 3.2 & 3.3)

#3.   Comparing Preferences and Daydreams (Objectives 3.4 & 3.5)

#4.   Researching Occupational Preferences (Objective 3:6)

#5.   Planning for Career Exploration (Objective 3.7)

Together, these five lesson plans comprise a unit dealing with the general objective "Formulates tentative career hypothesis". It's no more complex than that. Functional criteria are used to define what is a lesson and what is a unit. That is:

1.   The general level objective defines the parameters for each unit.

2.   Lesson plans are developed to facilitate specific level objectives.

3.   A lesson plan may be developed for a single objective or for multiple objectives depending upon commonality of objectives and preferences of the instructor.

4.   The time needed to instruct a lesson depends on the complexity of the objective(s), the nature and level of the learner, and the priorities of the instructor.

5.   A unit is composed of all lesson plans required to instruct the specific level objectives subsumed under one general level objective.

Units and lessons can stand alone and be instructed separately, or they may be fused with the existing curriculum. Common approaches to the implementation of career education are discussed in the next section.

## Approaches to Implementation

The process of lesson plan development has been emphasized in this chapter because career education requires the introduction of new objectives into the curriculum. How these objectives will be incorporated into the existing educational process will be the subject of this section. It cannot be emphasized too strongly that *there is no single best way to implement career education.* Rather, there are many different ways; each having specific strengths and weaknesses. With over 16,000 school districts in the United States, it is reasonable to expect wide variations in how education is prescribed, organized and conducted. Generally speaking, there are four common approaches to career education in current use. Each is described below.

### Subject Matter Enrichment

The bulk of American public and private education is centered around the teaching of subject matter. Four subjects are predominant: (a) mathematics, (b) science, (c) social studies, and (d) language arts/ English. Other subjects like art, music, physical education, foreign language, vocational education, etc. are also included depending upon state education requirements, grade level, local preferences and other factors.

A prominent approach to career education is called *infusion.* Earlier in Chapter Four this approach was characterized as the "secondary role" for career education. In practical terms this means using work-related topics, activities, materials and methods to teach existing subject matter concepts and skills. For example, using books about occupations in language arts class to teach reading. In this way, career education is used as a "means" to better accomplish an existing "end". This approach is most frequently found at the elementary school level and is the simplest to implement.

### Curriculum Implementation

The primary role for career education is to facilitate the career development aspect of general growth and learning. The curriculum model contained in the previous chapter describes the types of knowledges, attitudes and skills associated with career development. If career education is to achieve its purpose of reforming education, then these new objectives must be incorporated into the curriculum.

In some school districts career education is taught as a supplemental unit, mini-course, or course. A number of commercial publishing companies market complete semester-length and year-length programs. Such units or courses are taught by existing teachers or new, specially-trained career education teachers or coordinators.

The practice of teaching career education as a separate unit, mini-course or course may have disadvantages. Given an already over-crowded curriculum and severe budget limitations, most school districts simply cannot add additional subjects, courses and teachers. Instead most school districts integrate career education into existing programs or courses. This can be called a *fusion* approach since a career education objective is wedded to an existing academic objective and both are accomplished simultaneously. For example, a social studies objective dealing with developing "awareness of the role of responsible citizens in the consumption of goods" can be fused with a career education objective related to developing "awareness of occupations involved in the production of goods". Essentially the same topics and materials can be used to develop two different types of learning outcomes.

This practice is known as teaching toward multiple objectives. Unfortunately, too few teachers understand or apply this method. Many teachers confuse this method with the infusion method described earlier. The relationship between the infusion approach and the fusion approach is illustrated in Figure 5:2. Study the illustration and consider this discussion very carefully. The infusion approach is a valid and much needed improvement in the way students are taught. However, we must go beyond this method to also add new career education learner outcomes. This can be done by adding units and courses or by fusing career education with the existing curriculum. The latter approach is probably the more desirable alternative.

## Guidance and Counseling

This approach, like curriculum implementation, is designed to facilitate career development. The primary differences between the two are in: (a) who teaches it, and (b) the types of learning outcomes taught and the methods used.

As the name implies, this approach to career education is "taught" by guidance counselors. Historically, the educational preparation of guidance personnel has included some exposure to the

**Figure 5:2**

**RELATIONSHIP BETWEEN TWO APPROACHES TO CAREER EDUCATION IMPLEMENTATION**

**Infusion:** Career education as an instructional method to teach basic academic skills.

**Fusion:** Career education as both method and outcome; the wedding of career education objectives and basic academic skill objectives. Both accomplished simultaneously.

Academic skill objective

Career education topic, activity or method

Academic skill   +   Career education
objective                    objective

Career education topic, activity or method

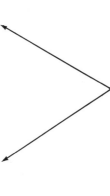

need for career guidance. In one sense, guidance personnel are better prepared to implement career education than existing elementary and secondary school teachers. Guidance counselors engage in the implementation of career education primarily: (a) by assisting the regular teacher via "itinerant" or team teaching in the classroom; (b) through group guidance activities specifically set aside for that purpose, often in homerooms or assembly halls; (c) through individualized instruction and individual counseling, and (d) by managing computer-assisted guidance and/or other methods that employ audio-visual equipment or other types of hardware.

A second way that the guidance and counseling approach may differ from curriculum implementation is in what is taught and how it's taught. Because of their education and training, guidance counselors are especially well equipped to assist students in learning *affective* types of outcomes. That is, those objectives concerned with feelings, emotions, values, self knowledge, and the like. Guidance counselors have an important role in the administration and interpretation of self assessment instruments, like those dealing with interests, abilities and values. The learning of decision-making and value-clarification skills are also ones with which guidance counselors can effectively deal.

## Community Partnerships

A major goal of career education is to involve community based organizations and individuals in "partnerships" to implement career education. Hoyt's 1980 article[8] is an excellent summary of the dozens of national organizations, corporations and education associations that endorsed career education and maintained formal working relationships with the federal Office of Career Education. The following thirteen national community organizations are included in this group:

1.  Association of Junior Leagues, Inc.
2.  American Legion
3.  American Legion Auxiliary
4.  Boy Scouts of America
5.  4-H Clubs of America
6.  Girl Scouts of the U.S.A.
7.  Goodwill Industries, Inc.
8.  American Association of Retired Persons
9.  Junior Achievement, Inc.

10.  Rotary International
11.  Women's American ORT
12.  National School Volunteers Program
13.  NBC's "Parents' Guide to Television"

Several examples may help to clarify how such groups can contribute to career education. Since 1976, professional staff persons from Girl Scouts of the USA (GSUSA) National Headquarters, have been developing and, with the assistance of various local Girl Scout Councils, field-testing a new career awareness/career exploration program called *From Dreams to Reality*. These materials consist of: (a) activity books, (b) career cards, (c) leader's guide, and (d) council guide. Each of the activities in the program are designed to fit into the informal kind of learning environment that typifies GSUSA troop meetings.[9]

Women's American ORT (Organization for Rehabilitation Through Training) is a national volunteer organization composed of approximately 135,000 American Jewish women. In the state of Florida WAO members have established the "Dade County Coalition for Career Education". This effort has resulted in drawing together a total of 15 influential community organizations to participate with the Dade County schools in a collaborative career education effort.[10]

A number of local Rotary Clubs, affiliated with Rotary International, are involved in career education. In Corpus Christi, Texas, Rotary members compiled a "Careers Resource Book" containing names of persons who are willing to work with teachers and pupils at the K-12 level. The listing includes about 1,200 persons from the business/industry community and is distributed, by Rotary, to all classroom teachers. Resource persons listed in the book visit elementary and secondary school classrooms to help students see relationships between what they study and the nature of various occupations.[11]

## Qualities for Career Education Curricula *

The curriculum model that was proposed in Chapter Four and the teaching methods suggested in this chapter are deliberately broader in scope than more narrowly defined "occupational information programs." The educational theory advocated in this book is known as *process education*.[12] Process education recognizes that the first and foremost objective of curriculum and instruction should be the

* The seven "Qualities for Career Education Curriculum" discussed in this section were originally proposed by Professor Henry P. Cole in 1973 while under contract to the *Career Development for Children Project* that was directed by the author.

facilitation of *skills* which learners need if they are to acquire, organize, generate, and utilize in a productive manner the wealth of information and knowledge available to them. More traditional content-oriented programs seem to be concerned only with having students learn a specific body of subject matter content. If the goals of a process-oriented career education curriculum are to be achieved, Cole[13] maintains that such a curriculum should possess the following seven qualities:

## Quality One

A capacity for dealing with change and an acceptance of uncertainty must be fostered. The curriculum should raise many questions about the future and the student's possible role in that future. It should present many issues to students for possible resolution, e.g., "What is work and what is play and what are the commonalities and differences between them?"; "Why is something that is work for one person play for another?" The curriculum should strive to achieve closure and consensus only on facts and empirical information. It should not encourage uniform consensus or closure on the multiple inferences and generalizations which can be produced from those facts.

## Quality Two

A basic fluency and flexibility of perception, feeling, thinking, expression, and action should be developed. Curriculum activities should never be designed to give the impression that there is only one way to define a term; to categorize events, people, occupations, or ideas; or to interpret a given set of empirical observations. Rather, the curriculum should present students with many opportunities to reorganize, reclassify, and reinterpret concepts, generalizations, methods, and stereotypes which are the content of any curriculum.

Furthermore, if the skill is deemed worth teaching, the curriculum should present opportunity for its use in many contexts. This quality can best be achieved by building a basic fluency within each activity in the curriculum. Each individual activity should require and ensure a variety of differing but logical responses from students individually or as a group. The practice should extend beyond a given activity since basic skills deemed essential in the curriculum are dealt with in a spiral fashion and in a new and increasingly diverse and complex situation as Bruner has suggested.[14, 15] This principle of curriculum organization is well recognized by many curriculum developers who seek to develop capacity for divergent thinking, problem solving, and expressive behavior.[16, 17]

## Quality Three

The curriculum must respect the questing, imaginative, and playful nature of the child. It should provide activities which ensure the retention of the basic motivation to quest for meaning. Torrance has noted from empirical evidence that excessive concentration of curriculum activities on developing convergency in thinking, interpretation, and operation causes a reduction in basic fluency and flexibility of action and thinking.[18] He has referred to this as the "fourth grade slump."[19] Many other scholars have noted similar patterns resulting from schooling.[20, 21]

The playful questing of the child can perhaps best be fostered if curriculum developers, teachers, and parents can themselves remain open to the idea that any process-organized curriculum need not be overly concerned with the content experiences a given child encounters or fails to encounter. If certain process skills are stated as objectives for a curriculum, and if these skills have a good rationale that justifies their selection for attention, then the curriculum must provide enough specific and varied topics, materials, and activities for students to engage in the use of skills that may be internalized, generalized, and broadened.

With such a process orientation, the content of particular curriculum activities and topics can be viewed as a sample of perhaps an infinite array of content that serves as a vehicle in developing the skills that are the stated outcomes. Concern whether or not all students have mastered particular content or concepts begins to take on less importance. The content of the curriculum becomes less of a sacred cow and the curriculum designer, teacher, and students are much more free to operate within a wide array of topics. It becomes an impossible task to teach for mastery of all content. It demoralizes students and teachers. There is simply too much to learn and too little reason for learning all that is known.

## Quality Four

The curriculum must provide students with many opportunities for them to be successful in solving problems, in clarifying their own values and meanings, and in recognizing ambiguities and ambivalence in their own beliefs and beliefs of others. The curriculum must develop the understanding about one's purpose and ideals. It must somehow develop a self-confidence in the student. Students must come to feel that they are effective problem-solvers and that they are equipped with the means to interpret situations in their lives productively and adaptively. The curriculum must present numerous opportunities for them to test their speculations and solutions to problems and to determine the consequences. If possible, the curriculum should provide opportunities and activities for students to conduct further testing of their views about self and others in non-school contexts.

## Quality Five

The curriculum must broadly inform the student about the diversity of beliefs, roles, and responsibilities in career activities of people. It should bring them in contact from early elementary years through high school years with a variety of persons who are currently working out their ideals and meeting their basic economic needs in their occupations. It should inform students of the role expectations which define the privileges and responsibilities of various occupational roles within career categories. It should provide students with the same means to categorize different occupational activities as being alike and different in the services and products rendered and the statuses, rewards, and sense of purpose achieved. It should develop the capacity of students to seek out and explore multiple ways in which they may meet their basic economic needs and their "being" needs through planning for career development within a given occupational family or across several related occupational families. The teacher of career education should recognize that much significant learning cannot and should not be confined to the classroom.

## Quality Six

The activities in a career development curriculum should develop a child's capacity for tolerance, compassion, and empathy. As Piaget and Kohlberg have pointed out, the process of maturing as a moral person is lifelong.[22] This skill is best defined as the ability to adopt other roles, to empathize with others toward better comprehending why people behave as they do in given situations. Stephens pointed out that some people never fully develop their moral capacity for tolerance and understanding.[23]

A good deal of the ability of children to develop to such a level is probably a function of the child-rearing procedures used with them by their parents and teachers. Singer and Singer present interesting generalizations based on empirical observations and studies which indicate that warm, permissive parents produce children who develop these types of moral characteristics as well as self-reliant, creative personalities.[24] Hostile, restrictive parents tend to develop fearful, anxious, self-destructive children. Hostile, permissive parents tend to develop children with strong identities who are self-reliant but are outwardly aggressive, hostile, and socially destructive. Warm, restrictive parents tend to develop children who are anxious, overcontrolled, achievement oriented and conforming. Although Singer and Singer make these generalizations primarily about the child-rearing practices of parents, it appears that teachers also can be globally categorized into one of the four quadrants of the two-dimensional paradigm for child rearing.

It seems clear that the type of creative, self-motivated, responsible and moral person called for as the product of career development curriculums is best socialized through the warm-permissive dimension. The career development curriculum should probably be designed to foster such an atmosphere. The teacher, of course, must also adopt such a view and implement it in the curriculum to achieve this goal. A curriculum designed to be warm and permissive toward students does not mean there would be no structure and planning. On the contrary, there should be a great deal of structure and extensive planning, much more so than in a typical narrow, prescriptive program.

A capacity for tolerance, compassion, and empathy probably contributes more to a person's ability to interact productively with his or her peers than any other set of skills. This set of basic skills is the cement which holds the matrix of any social organization together. The ability of a person to get along with others, to understand their acts and motives, to empathize with their feelings and values is probably more important in one's occupational role than in any other social situation with, perhaps, the exception of one's immediate family. Career development curriculums should incorporate many activities which foster the capacity for interpersonal regard.

## Quality Seven

The curriculum must help children find ways to contribute meaningfully to the welfare of some groups. Increased specialization and years of formal education have prolonged the period of economic dependence of children upon their parents. Many children have difficulty feeling that anything they do contributes in a significant way to the welfare of their family and community. Children, like all people, want to count for something. They want to be competent in some things and esteemed for their contribution. Some children satisfy these needs through their schoolwork, and school and community activities. Many other children fail to see the relevance of such activities to anything of significance or worth. Some encounter this problem at grade three, many others in junior high, high school, and some later. Minimally, the career development curriculum should provide ample opportunity for these feelings of anomy and purposelessness to be shared, examined, and discussed.

At best, activities in a career development curriculum should provide the means for students to generate ways and outlets for the contribution of their talents to some constructive cause, to explore and seek out ways to express fidelity. This is an acute problem. Bruner calls it the conflict between social and personal relevance.[25] He notes that, unfortunately, most of the curriculum which is perceived as being of great social relevance by educators and parents is at the same time perceived as being of little personal relevance by students. A career development curriculum could provide the means for students, teachers, and community leaders to deal with and attempt continuously to resolve this issue. It is an issue one can always rally a group of students to discuss. It is an issue which has no ultimate resolution. It is also an issue which continues lifelong in one's career activities.

Once again, it is the process for dealing with and adaptively resolving potential conflict between personal meaning and goals and social-organizational missions which should be the goal of instruction. It is not the convincing of the students or employees that the social relevance of their studying or working must have personal relevance for them because it is decreed somewhere by some great authority or principle.

These, then, are the basic qualities which career development curriculums must meet if they are to be consistent with the basic issues faced by our society in educating youth toward meaningful and personally satisfying career roles. While such qualities have been discussed within the context of career education, *they are qualities which are generally applicable to all of education at every grade level.*

## Evaluating Career Education Programs

One role for evaluation is to monitor student performance and collect data in order that judgments can be made about the extent to which learning is taking place. Thus, evaluation is a very important part of the teaching-learning process. This role for evaluation was discussed earlier within the context of the four-step method of teaching.

Another important role for evaluation is that of program improvement. Mitchell[26] defines evaluation as ". . . a process designed to provide data for management decisions both during and after implementation of an activity. The focus is not solely on proving (product or outcome evaluation) but also on improving, particularly during the first full cycle of implementation." The program is the object of the evaluation rather than the learner.

Since its inception in the early 1970s, concerns have been prominent relative to evaluating the effectiveness of career education.

Hoyt[27] notes that ". . . never has such a small program, within the United States Office of Education, devoted so much attention to evaluating its effectiveness on such a sustained basis as has been true for career education." Rather than attempt to discuss a subject as comprehensive as evaluation, the reader is referred to the following reports, monographs and articles. They provide more than adequate treatment of models, methods, and instruments for evaluating career education programs.

Tuckman, B.W. and Carducci, J.A. *Evaluating Career Education: A Review and Model.* Report No. 36. National Institute of Education (DHEW). Washington, D.C.: U.S. Government Printing Office, 1974. (ED 102 212)

Development Associates, Inc. *Handbook for the Evaluation of Career Education Programs.* Washington, D.C.: U.S. Office of Education; August 1974. (ED 099 682)

Development Associates, Inc. *An Evaluation of Vocational Exemplary Projects: Part D, Vocational Education Act Amendments of 1968.* Prepared for the Division of Vocational and Technical Education, U.S. Office of Education, March 1975. (ED 109 475)

Development Associates, Inc. *Evaluation and Educational Decision Making: A Functional Guide to Evaluating Career Education.* Washington, D.C.: U.S. Office of Education: September 1975. (ED 117 185)

Enderlein, T. *A Review of Career Education Evaluation Studies.* Washington, D.C.: U.S. Government Printing Office, 1976. (ED 141 584)

Hoyt, K.B. *Perspectives on the Problem of Evaluation in Career Education.* Washington, D.C.: U.S. Government Printing Office, 1976. (ED 127 471)

"Focus on Evaluation of Career Education." *Journal of Career Education* 1976, 2 (3).

National Advisory Council for Career Education, *The Efficacy of Career Education.* Washington, D.C.: U.S. Government Printing Office, 1976. (ED 130 092)

Bhaerman, R.D. *Career Education and Basic Academic Achievement: A Descriptive Analysis of the Research.* Washington, D.C.: U.S. Government Printing Office, 1977. (ED 140 032)

Datta, Lois-ellin et al. *Career Education What Proof Do We Have That It Works?* Washington, D.C.: U.S. Government Printing Office, 1977. (ED 151 516)

Bonnett, D.G. *Evaluation Design and Reporting in Career Education.* Washington, D.C.: U.S. Government Printing Office, 1978.

Mitchell, A.A. *Evaluating Career Education: Some Practical Models.* Salt Lake City, Utah: Olympus Publishing Company, 1979.

"Evaluating the Elusive Aspects of Career Education." *Journal of Research and Development in Education,* 1979, 12 (3).

*Career Education Measurement Series.* Columbus, Ohio: National Center for Research in Vocational Education:

"Assessing Experiential Learning in Career Education," R & D Series No. 165, 1979. (ED 183 875)

"Career Education Measures. A Compendium of Evaluation Instruments," R & D Series No. 166, 1979. (ED 183 876)

"A Guide for Improving Locally Developed Career Education Measures," R & D Series No. 167, 1979. (ED 183 879)

"Improving the Accountability of Career Education Programs: Evaluation Guidelines and Checklists," R & D Series No. 168, 1979. (ED 183 878)

"Using Systematic Observation Techniques in Evaluating Career Education," R & D Series No. 169, 1979. (ED 183 879)

Hoyt, K.B. *Evaluation of K-12 Career Education: A Status Report.* Washington, D.C.: U.S. Government Printing Office, 1980. (ED 189 394)

"Career Education" In *Encyclopedia of Educational Research, Volume 1.* New York: The Free Press, 1982, pp. 231-241.

## Summary

The implementation of career education does not necessitate radical reform. It does, however, require some degree of change. If present schools were adequately helping students to "learn about and prepare to engage in work," then, there would be no reason for the career education movement to exist.

This chapter has illustrated how tested principles of curriculum and instruction can be applied to the successful implementation of career education. Installing the career education concept into a local K-12 school is not significantly different than implementing any new innovation. The same barriers to change exist; the same gateways to change exist. The single most important variable in changing education is the quality and commitment of administrators and faculty. This book was written for practitioners in recognition of their prime role in career education.

### REFERENCES

1. Bailey, L. J. "Curriculum for Career Development Education," In J. Schaffarzick and D. Hampson, *Strategies for Curriculum Development.* Berkeley, California: McCutchan, 1975, pp. 185-210.

2. *Career Education Programs That Work.* Washington, D.C.: U.S. Government Printing Office, September 1979.

3. *It's Working... Collaboration in Career Education.* Washington, D.C.: U.S. Government Printing Office, March 1979.

4. High, S.C., Jr. "Collaboration Between the National Diffusion Network and OCE", *Journal of Career Education,* 1980, 7 (2), 161-166.

5. Kaplan, C.B. and Hamilton, J.A. "Seeking JDRP Approval: Answers to Common Questions of Career Education Practitioners". *Journal of Career Education,* 1980, 7 (2), 167-174.

6. Krathwohl, D.R. "Stating Objectives Appropriately for Program, for Curriculum, and for Instructional Material Development," *Journal of Teacher Education,* 1965, 16, 83-92.

7. Cole, H.P. *Approaches to the Logical Validation of Career Development Curriculum Paradigms.* Carbondale, Illinois: Southern Illinois University, Career Development for Children Project, 1973.

8. Hoyt, K.B. "Career Education: A Report Card for the 70s and Some Predictions for the Decade of the 1980s", *Journal of Career Education,* 1980, 7 (2), 82-96.

9. Hoyt, K.B. *Exploring Division Boy Scouts of America, Girl Scouts of the U.S.A., and Career Education.* Washington, D.C.: U.S. Government Printing Office, 1978.

10. Hoyt, K.B. *Women's American ORT and Career Education.* Washington, D.C.: U.S. Government Printing Office, 1978.

11. Hoyt, K.B. *Rotary International and Career Education.* Washington, D.C.: U.S. Government Printing Office, 1978.

12. Cole, H.P. *Process Education: The New Direction for Elementary-Secondary Schools.* Englewood Cliffs, New Jersey: Educational Technology Publications, 1972.

13. Ibid.

14. Bruner, J.S. *The Process of Education.* New York: Random House, 1960.

15. Bruner, J.S. *Toward a Theory of Instruction.* New York: W.W. Norton, 1968.

16. Torrance, E.P. *Rewarding Creative Behavior.* Englewood Cliffs, New Jersey: Prentice-Hall, 1965.

17. Williams, F.E. (Ed.) *Creativity at Home and in School.* St. Paul, Minnesota: Macalester Creativity Project, 1968.

18. Torrance, 1965.

19. Torrance, E.P. "A Longitudinal Examination of the Fourth Grade Slump in Creativity", *The Gifted Child Quarterly,* 1968, 12 (4), 195-199.

20. Williams, 1968.

21. Mackinnon, D.W. "The Courage to Be: Realizing Creative Potential." In L.J. Rubin, (Ed.), *Life Skills in School and Society.* Washington, D.C.: Association for Supervision and Curriculum Development, NEA, 1969.

22. Stephens, J.M. *The Psychology of Classroom Learning.* New York: Holt, Rinehart and Winston, 1965.

23. Ibid.

24.     Singer, R.D. and Singer, A. *Psychological Development in Children.* Phila-
        delphia, Pennsylvania: W. B. Saunders Co., 1969.

25.     Bruner, 1968.

26.     Mitchell, A.M. *Evaluating Career Education: Some Practical Models.* Salt
        Lake City, Utah: Olympus Publishing Company, 1979, p. 3.

27.     Hoyt, K.B. *Evaluation of K-12 Career Education: A Status Report.* Wash-
        ington, D.C.: U.S. Government Printing Office, 1980.

# APPENDIX

# APPENDIX A

---

## APPLICATION OF LESSON PLANNING FUNDAMENTALS

1. Blank Lesson plan form (pages 162 and 163)

2. Sample, completed lesson plan for goal A1 (pages 166 and 167)

3. Sample, completed lesson plan for goal D2 (pages 170-176)

4. Sample, completed unit and five individual lesson plans for goal C1 (pages 179-198)

NOTE: The examples provided here were developed to illustrate the process of lesson plan development. They are intended to serve as prototypes for others to follow. No endorsement of commercially produced materials used in the lessons is intended or implied.

159

# BLANK LESSON PLAN FORM

## LESSON PLAN FORM: PART I

Goal _____

    Lesson Plan # _____ Grade Level _____

    LESSON TITLE _____

A.    General Objective (unit theme)

B.    Specific Objective(s)

C.    Instructional Materials, Supplies, and Equipment

D.    Unique Learner Needs or Characteristics

# LESSON PLAN FORM: PART II

| Periods | Est. Time | |
|---------|-----------|---|
| | | 1. *Preparation Step* |
| | | 2. *Presentation Step* |
| | | 3. *Application Step* |
| | | 4. *Evaluation Step* |

# SAMPLE, COMPLETED LESSON PLAN FOR GOAL A1

Goal       A1.   Becoming Aware of Self Characteristics

---

Lesson Plan # 4                           Grade Level    1

---

LESSON TITLE       Being Alike and Different

---

A.    General Objective (unit theme)

      1.    Forms generalizations about self

B.    Specific Objective(s)

      1.4    Recognizes uniqueness of own self

C.    Instructional Materials, Supplies and Equipment

      1.    *The Joy of Being You,* filmstrip/cassette and Teaching Guide
         (Scholastic-Kindle)

      2.    Filmstrip projector

      3.    Twenty-five *About Me* booklets (Houghton Mifflin)

      4.    Shelf paper and felt tip pen (activity 1.1)

      5.    Weight scale and measuring tape (activity 3.1)

      6.    Twenty-five 11 x 13 sheets of construction paper, students use own
         supplies (activity 3.3)

      7.    Twenty-five 8½ x 11 sheets of paper (activity 4.1)

D.    Unique Learner Needs or Characteristics

      Class is normal in achievement and in physical and psychological
      characteristics

| Periods | Est. Time | |
|---|---|---|
| | | 1. *Preparation Step* |
| 2 | 30 min. | 1.1 Cut shelf paper to length of each child. Place paper on table or floor and have child lie on it. Trace outline with felt tip marker. Have child draw in features, clothing, etc. Display in classroom. |
| | | or |
| 1 | 30 min. | 1.2 Have students bring snapshots of themselves to display on bulletin board. |
| | | 2. *Presentation Step* |
| 1 | 20 min. | 2.1 (Review Teacher Guide.) View filmstrip. |
| 1 | 30 min. | 2.2 Discuss questions 4, 6, 7, and 10 in Teacher Guide. |
| | | 3. *Application Step* |
| 2 | 30 min. | 3.1 Have children measure and record their height and weight. Chart information on board in graph form. Let children find themselves on the chart. (Be alert that kids on exteme ends of the scale do not develop negative feelings about themselves). |
| 6 | 20 min. | 3.2 Complete workbooks. |
| 1 | 30 min. | 3.3 On large sheets of construction paper, have children print "Things I Like to Do." Have them cut out pictures from magazines or draw pictures of work and play activities they enjoy doing. |
| | | 4. *Evaluation Step* |
| 1 | 20 min. | 4.1 Have children mark or fold paper into fourths. Have them list or illustrate four characteristics that make them unique. |

Example

# SAMPLE, COMPLETED LESSON
# PLAN FOR GOAL D2

## LESSON PLAN FORM

Goal   D2. Executing plans to qualify for post-high school career objectives

Lesson Plan #  10                          Grade Level   10

LESSON TITLE   Owning a Small Business

A.   General Objective (unit theme)

  2.   Explores occupational clusters to validate occupational preferences and to develop new knowledge and skills.

B.   Specific Objective(s)

  2.6   Shows awareness of the nature of small business ownership.

C.   Instructional Materials, Supplies, and Equipment

  1.   Article on "Working for Yourself: What's It Like," *Occupational Outlook Quarterly,* 1973, 17(1), 20-30, (20 copies).

  2.   Activity Sheet "Identifying Work Tasks," (20 copies).

  3.   Activity sheet "Advantages and Disadvantages," (20 copies).

  4.   Optional activity sheet "Interview Guide," (20 copies)

  5.   *New Entrepreneur* film, (ACI Films, Inc.).

D.   Unique Learner Needs or Characteristics

  Class is above average in aptitude and ability. Majority seem interested in pursuing post-high school education or training. Several in class have been outspoken about the "system" which they perceive to be anti-individual.

## LESSON PLAN FORM *(cont.)*

| Periods | Est. Time | |
|---|---|---|
| (50 min. periods) | | 1. *Preparation Step* |
| | 2 min. | 1.1. Introduce this lesson by noting that students have been exploring various occupational clusters, but primarily in terms of what an employee does. |
| | 3 min. | 1.2 Point out that thousands of people work for themselves (i.e., they own their own business) and in addition may be *employers* of others. Explain that the purpose of this lesson is to introduce students to what it might be like to own and operate a small business. |
| | | 2. *Presentation Step* |
| | 8 min. | 2.1 Place on the board the word en-tre-pre-neur and ask if anyone knows what it means. Explain that entrepreneur is a French word referring to "a person who organizes and manages a business undertaking." Ask students to identify various types of entrepreneurs. |
| 1 | 2 min. | 2.2 Provide additional orientation to the topic by explaining that the term "small business" means many different things — especially for government purposes. The way in which small business will be used in the lesson is to refer to companies which are owned and operated by only one to five people. |
| | 15 min. | 2.3 Pass out the short article "Working for Yourself: What's It Like," and have students read it. Explain that the article is a case study of a day in the life of a small business owner. |
| | 20 min. | 2.4 After everyone has read the article discuss the following questions: |
| | | a. Independence is often given as a major reason for owning a business. Is the small business owner really independent? (Consider how many persons the business owner depends on and how many persons depend on him or her.) |

## LESSON PLAN FORM *(cont.)*

| Periods | Est. Time |
|---|---|
| | |
| 2 | 50 min. |
| 3 | 50 min. |
| 4 | 50 min. |
| | |
| | |
| 5 | 50 min. |

b. Given the same type of job, would you rather work for someone else for 40 hours a week at $400, or work for yourself for 50-60 hours at $400? Why or why not?

c. What type of person do you think would make a good entrepreneur?

2.5 View the film "New Entrepreneur." Discuss how Denise Cobb (in the film) and Len Kirsten are alike. Do you think there are any differences in small business opportunities for males and females?

3. *Application Step*

3.1 To illustrate the many types of roles in which an entrepreneur engages, have students complete the activity sheet entitled "Identifying Work Tasks." Discuss the results and summarize findings on the board.

3.2 To illustrate that small business ownership involves both advantages and disadvantages, have students complete the activity sheet entitled "Advantages and Disadvantages." Discuss with the class. Keep in mind, however, that advantages and disadvantages are relative terms depending upon each person's perspective.

3.3 (optional) If students seem to be particularly interested in this lesson, use the activity sheet entitled "Interview Guide" and have them complete it outside of class. Later, have students compare and discuss their findings.

4. *Evaluation Step*

4.1 Since this lesson is primarily motivational and informational, no separate evaluation is conducted.

4.2 By way of concluding this lesson, invite a representative of the *Small Business Administration* to come to class and discuss the services and publications of SBA. Encourage interested students to write for free SBA information and literature.

## ACTIVITY SHEET LESSON D2-10

### IDENTIFYING WORK TASKS

Instructions: In his role as a small business owner, Len Kirsten performs many different work tasks. In a large organization, such work tasks would probably be performed by a single person. Following is an example of what is meant. Add as many job tasks and job titles to this list as you can think of.

**Job Task**                                    **Job Title**

1. Supervises employees                    Sales Manager

2. _____                  _____

3. _____                  _____

4. _____                  _____

5. _____                  _____

6. _____                  _____

7. _____                  _____

8. _____                  _____

9. _____                  _____

10. _____                 _____

11. _____                 _____

12. _____                 _____

(Use additional pages if needed)

## ACTIVITY SHEET LESSON D2-10

## ADVANTAGES AND DISADVANTAGES

Instructions: In the space below, list as many advantages and disadvantages as you can of being a small business owner.

**Advantages**                              **Disadvantages**

1. _____        _____

2. _____        _____

3. _____        _____

4. _____        _____

5. _____        _____

6. _____        _____

7. _____        _____

8. _____        _____

9. _____        _____

10. _____       _____

In your opinion, do the advantages outweigh the disadvantages? Record your answer below.

_____

_____

_____

## ACTIVITY SHEET LESSON D2-10

### INTERVIEW GUIDE

Instructions: Select a small business owner in your community. Interview him/ her to gain a better idea of the working conditions of small business owners. Use the following questions as a guide in your interview.

1. Name of business _____

2. What goods are sold, or what services are provided?_____

_____

3. How many full-time people are employed?\_\_\_\_\_Part-time employees?\_\_\_\_\_ Are there any other people who are employed on an occcasional basis (attorney, bookkeeper)? _____

_____

4. What are the six most important job tasks that you perform?

_____     _____

_____     _____

_____     _____

5. What type of *educational* background did you have before you started this

business? _____

_____

6. What type of *work experience* background did you have before you started

this business? _____

_____

7. Which was more valuable, the educational experience or the work experience?

_____ Why?_____

_____

8. Have you taken any additional educational courses or training since opening the business? _____ If so, what kind? _____

_____

9. How many hours do you work each week? _____ How much vacation time do you have each year? _____

10. What three things do you like most about your business?

_____

_____

_____

11. What three things do you like the least?

_____

_____

_____

12. If you had to do it over again, would you do the same thing? _____

_____

_____

13. Use the additional space below for your own questions and comments.

SAMPLE, COMPLETED UNIT AND

FIVE LESSON PLANS FOR GOAL C1

# LESSON PLAN FORM

Goal      C1. Clarifying Occupational Self Concept

Lesson Plan #  1                    Grade Level  8

LESSON TITLE    SDS Assessment

A.   General Objective (unit theme)

   3.    Formulates tentative career hypotheses

B.   Specific Objective(s)

   3.1    Completes SDS assessment booklet

C.   Instructional Materials, Supplies, and Equipment

   1.    *The Self Directed Search, Form E* (one copy per student).

   2.    "Professional Manual" and "Counselor's Guide" for instructor use.

   3.    (Note: Students should use pencils to facilitate making corrections.)

D.   Unique Learner Needs or Characteristics

Three classes will complete this unit with a total enrollment of 58 (22-19-17). Males and females are approximately equally represented. All students are at least average in scholastic aptitude. However, about half of them are weak in verbal and writing skills.

All students have previously been introduced to the 15 occupational cluster areas. All students have used the *Occupational Outlook Handbook* at least once, but none extensively.

## LESSON PLAN FORM *(cont.)*

| Periods | Est. Time | |
|---|---|---|
| (40 min. periods) | | 1. *Preparation Step* |
| | | 1.1 (Review "Professional Manual" and "A Counselor's Guide) |
| | 5 min. | 1.2 Introduce this lesson by explaining to students that they are going to complete a short booklet which is designed to help them collect information which they can use in making future career plans. Emphasize that the activity is *not* a test and they will not be graded. |
| | 5 min. | 1.3 Review the need to make a choice of a high school curriculum and the importance of formulating tentative educational and occupational goals. |
| 1 | 10 min. | 1.4 Review the meaning of "interests" and "abilities." Point out that the booklet will assess their interests and abilities in addition to their preferences for different occupations. |
| | | 2. *Presentation Step* |
| | 5 min. | 2.1 Pass out copies of the SDS booklet and have students record name on front. |
| | | 2.2 Ask class to follow your instruction as each section of the booklet is completed. Direct students to proceed in the following manner: |
| | 15 min. | a. Page 3, list the five jobs which you might like to do. |
| | 10 min. | b. Pages 4 and 5, indicate your preferences for six kinds of activities. |
| | 10 min. | c. Pages 6 and 7, record your competency in six areas. |
| 2 | 10 min. | d. Pages 8 and 9, indicate your preferences for six kinds of occupations. |
| | 10 min. | e. Page 10, estimate your abilities for six areas. |
| | 5 min. | f. Pages 4-9, go back and total your scores for each page. |

## LESSON PLAN FORM *(cont.)*

| Periods | Est. Time | |
|---------|-----------|---|
| | 15 min. | g. Pages 11 and 12, complete graphs according to instructions. |
| 3 | 15 min. | h. Page 13, calculate summary score. |
| | | i. Page 13, record two-digit summary code. |
| | 5 min. | j. Have students recheck their arithmetic. (Note: Instructor should be familiar with how to deal with tied scores.) |

3. *Application Step*

3.1 Now that the mechanical part of recording information and calculating ratings is completed, it is a good idea to pause and query students about what has been accomplished.

3.2 Call on individual students to explain how each of the four summary ratings at the top of page 13 was obtained. (Caution students not to be concerned yet about the meaning of the six alphabet letters.) — 10 min.

3.3 Note that the ratings at the top of page 13 includes a self rating of abilities, and responses to questions related to likes, competencies, and jobs. Ask students to explain why they think four types of assessments were made rather than only one. — 10 min.

3.4 Ask students which types of data they think are more reliable: (a) verbal responses, or (b) written responses to specific categories of questions. Relate responses to what SDS seeks to accomplish. — 10 min.

3.5 Clarify any questions or concerns students may have about the SDS thus far. — 10 min.

4. *Evaluation Step*

4.1 Because of the potential to make procedural or arithmetic errors, this activity should be closely monitored. Circulate among the class as individual parts of the booklet are completed.

## LESSON PLAN FORM *(cont.)*

| Periods | Est. Time | |
|---------|-----------|--|
| | | 4.2 Collect booklets at this point. Quickly peruse all booklets to identify individuals who may have had difficulty. |
| | variable | 4.3 Provide individual tutoring as required. |

## LESSON PLAN FORM

Goal       C1.   Clarifying Occupational Self Concept

           Lesson Plan #   2              Grade Level   8

           LESSON TITLE    The Meaning of Summary Codes

A.    General Objective (unit theme)

     3.     Formulates tentative career hypotheses

B.    Specific Objective(s)

     3.2    Interprets meaning of SDS summary code

     3.3    Identifies ten occupations related to summary code

C.    Instructional Materials, Supplies, and Equipment

     1.     Completed SDS booklets.

     2.     *The Jobs Finder, Form E* (one copy per student).

     3.     "Professional Manual" and "Counselor's Guide."

     4.     Optional teacher-developed activity sheets re steps 2.3 and 4.2.

D.    Unique Learner Needs or Characteristics

Three classes will complete this unit with a total enrollment of 58 (22-19-17). Males and females are approximately equally represented. All students are at least average in scholastic aptitude. However, about half of them are weak in verbal and writing skills.

All students have previously been introduced to the 15 occupational cluster areas. All students have used the *Occupational Outlook Handbook* at least once, but none extensively.

## LESSON PLAN FORM *(cont.)*

| Periods | Est. Time | |
|---------|-----------|---|
| | 3 min. | 1. *Preparation Step* |
| | | 1.1 Begin by recalling that in the previous lesson students completed a series of exercises in the SDS booklet which culminated on page 13 with a two-letter code which symbolized their ability ratings and their responses in relation to likes, competencies, and job. |
| | 2 min. | 1.2 Explain that the present lesson will deal with interpreting the meaning of the summary code and with using the summary code as an aid to identifying preferred occupations. |
| | | 2. *Presentation Step* |
| | 1 min. | 2.1 Pass out SDS booklets which were collected after previous lesson and ask students to turn to page 14. |
| 1 | 3 min. | 2.2 Have students record their two-letter summary code from page 13 at the top of page 14. |
| | 1 min. | 2.3 Now, pass out *The Jobs Finder* and refer students to the top of page 2. |
| | 20 min. | 2.4 Write on the board (or prepare a handout sheet), and explain the meaning of the SDS groupings: Realistic (R) Investigative (I) Artistic (A) Social (S) Enterprising (E) Conventional (C) |
| | 10 min. | 2.4 Explain the meaning of students' two-letter summary code by relating them to the six SDS categories. Use two or three examples for illustration. |
| | 20 min. | 2.5 Next, using their "jobs finder," have students complete part 1 on page 14 by identifying and recording five occupations related to their summary code. |

## LESSON PLAN FORM *(cont.)*

| Periods | Est. Time | |
|---------|-----------|---|
| 2 | | |
| | 20 min. | 2.6 Repeat above procedure for part 2 on page 14. (Note: Instructor should review last paragraph on page 8 of the "Counselor's Guide" re steps 2.5 and 2.6) |
| | | 3. *Application Step* |
| | | 3.1 The SDS approach to educational and occupational planning is based on the assumption that *both* individual personalities *and* individual occupations can be classified with respect to six groupings: R-I-A-S-E-C. It is important here to apply students' understanding of the six groupings. |
| 3 | 10 min. | 3.2 Call on individuals to explain in their own words the meaning of each of the six SDS codes. |
| | 15 min. | 3.3 Have students interpret the meaning of their own two-letter summary code. |
| | 15 min. | 3.4 Finally, ask students to evaluate the extent to which their summary code describes their personality. Students should be encouraged to recall the findings from previous self-appraisal instruments and activities. The instructor could also select several individuals in the class to orally explain their summary code and ask the class if they think the summary description is a good characterization of their peer's personality type. |
| | | 4. *Evaluation Step* |
| | 5 min. | 4.1 Have students recheck parts 1 and 2 on page 14 to make sure the occupations they have listed are related to their two-letter summary code. |
| | 20 min. | 4.2 Place on the board (or duplicate an activity sheet) which contains 5 two-letter codes and 5 occupations, e.g., |

## LESSON PLAN FORM *(cont.)*

| Periods | Est. Time | |
|---|---|---|
| 4 | | **Summary Codes**        **Occupations** |

RS _____ Mechanical Engineer _____
IR _____ Interior Decorator    _____
EC _____ Dental Assistant      _____
CI _____ Gas Station Manager _____
SR _____ History Teacher       _____

Ask students to identify related occupations (column 1) and summary codes (column 2) respectively using the "jobs finder."

15 min.    4.3 Call to the students' attention the fact that some two-letter codes in the "jobs finder" (e.g., RA, IC, EA) have only a few occupations listed. Ask them to speculate why this is so.

variable    4.4 All students should have mastered understanding of the summary codes and use of the "jobs finder" before moving on to the next lesson. Provide tutorial assistance to any individual who may require it.

## LESSON PLAN FORM

Goal      C1. Clarifying Occupational Self Concept

Lesson Plan #   3                    Grade Level   8

LESSON TITLE    Comparing Preferences and Daydreams

A.   General Objective (unit theme)

   3.   Formulates tentative career hypotheses

B.   Specific Objective(s)

   3.4   Compares summary code occupations to "occupational daydreams."

   3.5   Given outcome of previous objective, prepares revised list of occupational preferences

C.   Instructional Materials, Supplies, and Equipment

   1.   Completed SDS booklets and "jobs finder."

   2.   "Professional Manual" and "Counselor's Guide."

   3.   Optional teacher-developed activity sheets re steps 2.3 and 4.2.

D.   Unique Learner Needs or Characteristics

   Three classes will complete this unit with a total enrollment of 58 (22-17-19). Males and females are approximately equally represented. All students are at least average in scholastic aptitude. However, about half of them are weak in verbal and writing skills.

   All students have previously been introduced to the 15 occupational cluster areas. All students have used the *Occupational Outlook Handbook* at least once, but none extensively.

## LESSON PLAN FORM *(cont.)*

| Periods | Est. Time | |
|---------|-----------|---|
| | | 1.  *Preparation Step* |
| | 3 min. | 1.1 Begin by recalling that in the previous lesson students used their two-letter summary codes to identify ten occupations which are assumed to be related to their "personality." |
| | 2 min. | 1.2 Explain that in the present lesson they will compare the ten occupations they identified on page 14 of the SDS with the 5 occupations they listed prior to completing the SDS self sppraisal. Next, they will prepare a revised list of 5 occupations which they will investigate in depth. |
| | | 2.  *Presentation Step* |
| | 10 min. | 2.1 Have students turn to page 3 of the SDS booklet and remind them that the five occupations listed were the ones they identified prior to using the SDS. Using their "jobs finder" have them write in the margin of page 3 the summary codes for the five occupations listed. |
| 1 | 15 min. | 2.2 Next, students should compare the two sets of occupational preferences, i.e., "before" (p. 3) and "after" (p. 14). Most students will find general agreement between their earlier aspirations and the SDS summary occupations. Sufficient class time and tutorial assistance should be provided at this step to assure that students understand the meaning of the comparisons they have made here. |
| | 10 min. | 2.3 Based on the outcome of the previous step, each student will prepare a revised list of five occupations which result from the SDS appraisal and from comparison and evaluation of aspirations made prior to using the SDS. |
| | | 2.4 The student has now "clarified his or her occupational self concept." The SDS booklets should be filed by the teacher or counselor for possible later use. Each student should record for use in |

## LESSON PLAN FORM *(cont.)*

| Periods | Est. Time | |
|---------|-----------|---|
| | | the next lesson the five occupations which summarize their current occupational preferences. |
| | | 3. *Application Step* |
| 2 | 40 min. | 3.1 Students should clearly understand the difference between how they arrived at their listing of occupations on p. 3 and p. 14. The following questions should be asked to stimulate discussion: |
| | | (a) What was the basis for your deciding on your earlier "occupational daydreams" (p. 3)? |
| | | (b) To what extent were your earlier aspirations based on self knowledge and occupational information? |
| | | (c) Was it difficult to think of five occupations to list on page 3? |
| | | (d) Did you have any difficulty identifying related occupations in the "jobs finder" after you knew your summary code? |
| | | (e) How compatible are your "occupational daydreams" and your SDS summary code occupations? |
| | | (f) What is your opinion of the SDS booklet and procedures? Was it worthwhile? Did you learn anything? Do you think you will be better equipped to make future decisions as a result of the SDS activity? |
| | | 4. *Evaluation Step* |
| | variable | 4.1 Some students may find that their "occupational daydreams" and their summary code occupations are completely dissimilar. Such students should be provided with individual assistance in completing steps 2.2 and 2.3 (Note: The instructor might find it helpful to review pp. 7-8 of the "professional manual" at this point.) |
| | (optional 15 min.) | 4.2 On page 7 of the "professional manual" a rating form is illustrated which allows students to rate |

**LESSON PLAN FORM** *(cont.)*

| Periods | Est. Time | |
|---|---|---|

the degree of agreement between their "occupational daydreams" and their summary code occupations. An adaptation of this rating scale could be prepared by the teacher for students to use. This is an optional activity which is probably unsuited for less mature students or ones who by visual inspection appear to have little agreement between preferences and "daydreams."

# LESSON PLAN FORM

Goal  C1. Clarifying Occupational Self Concept

    Lesson Plan # 4      Grade Level 8

    LESSON TITLE Researching Occupational Preferences

A. General Objective (unit theme)

  3. Formulates tentative career hypotheses

B. Specific Objective(s)

  3.6 Collects information about occupational preferences

C. Instructional Materials, Supplies, and Equipment

  1. Students' lists of occupational preferences.

  2. *Occupational Outlook Handbook,* most recent edition.

  3. Optional teacher-developed activity sheets re steps 2.1 and 2.3.

D. Unique Learner Needs or Characteristics

  Three classes will complete this unit with a total enrollment of 58 (22-19-17). Males and females are approximately equally represented. All students are at least average in scholastic aptitude. However, about half of them are weak in verbal and writing skills.

  All students have previously been introduced to the 15 occupational cluster areas. All students have used the *Occupational Outlook Handbook* at least once, but none extensively.

## LESSON PLAN FORM *( cont.)*

| Periods | Est. Time | |
|---|---|---|
| | | 1.  *Preparation Step* |
| | 3 min. | 1.1 Begin by recalling that the previous lesson culminated in students' having prepared a revised list of five occupations for which they have established a tentative preference. |
| | 2 min. | 1.2 Explain that in the present lesson students will research these occupations and collect data which can be used to develop more accurate career goals. |
| | (each student requires about 2 hours) | 2.  *Presentation Step*<br>(Note: the following activities can be done individually or with a group. A wide variety of occupational resources can be utilized. This lesson plan was developed with the intention that students would collect the required information during their non-class periods. *The Occupational Outlook Handbook* will be used as the prime reference material. Students have previously been instructed in the use of the *OOH*.) |
| 1 | 35 min. | 2.1 Instruct students that over the next two weeks they are to collect information about each of the five occupations they have identified. The following information should be collected about each occupation (a suitable date collection form can be easily designed and duplicated for student use):<br>a.  A short summary in students' own words about the "Nature of the Work" involved in that occupation.<br>b.  In what type of establishments do such people work (e.g., factories, hospitals, offices, banks)?<br>c.  Is the occupation primarily related to one cluster (e.g., construction, health) or is the occupation found in many or all clusters?<br>d.  What type of education or training do people in that occupation need?<br>e.  Is the occupation likely to *grow* or *decline* in the years ahead? |

## LESSON PLAN FORM *(cont.)*

| Periods | Est. Time | |
|---|---|---|
| | | 2.2 After students collect the required information they can be re-assembled for group instruction. |
| | | 3. *Application Step* |
| 2 | 10 min. | 3.1 Now, have students peruse the information they have collected and consider the following questions:<br>a. Is the "Nature of the Work" the same as you thought before? Are any of the work tasks involved similar for all five occupations?<br>b. Are the five occupations similar or dissimilar in terms of where people work?<br>c. What clusters are represented by the five occupations?<br>d. How compatible are the five occupations in terms of required education or training?<br>e. Are the occupations you studied ones which are going to grow or decline in the years ahead? |
| | 30 min. | 3.2 The previous questions are of the type which should help students to critically evaluate and interpret the data they have collected. These questions can be discussed in a large group, among a small group of peers, or individually between student and instructor. |
| 3 | 40 min. | 3.3 The final part of this step will be for students to synthesize their information in light of the above questions. Ask students to organize their responses to each of the following questions.<br>a. The five occupations I have studied are *similar* in the following ways _____.<br>b. The five occupations I have studied are *dissimilar* in the following ways _____.<br><br>This sheet should be attached with other information from this lesson and collected by the instructor. |

## LESSON PLAN FORM *(cont.)*

| Periods | Est. Time | |
|---------|-----------|---|
| | | 4. *Evaluation Step* |

4.1 It is recommended that the instructor peruse students' responses to the prior question and be prepared to provide feedback to them. It is unlikely that students at this age will be able to identify all of the similarities and differences which probably exist with respect to the five occupations they have studied. Nor, in all likelihood, will students fully comprehend the meanings of such similarities and differences.

*(Periods: 4   Est. Time: 40 min.)*

4.2 The instructor should select 2 or 3 student papers or develop case studies which illustrate several different patterns of findings. For example:

    a.   Student X has discovered that all of his or her occupations are related to the health cluster and require a college degree.

    b.   Student Y has selected all occupations where people work in offices. Such office occupations, however, are found in a number of different cluster areas.

    c.   Student Z doesn't seem to have established any real patterns in terms of educational level, types of cluster, and the like. This suggests that he or she will probably want to do a great deal more exploration.

4.3 Discuss these case studies or examples with students to illustrate the possible meanings of the data students have collected. Such discussions shall be intended to reinforce those students who are growing in self knowledge and who are demonstrating consistency in identifying occupational preferences. Similarly, students who exhibit a greater divergence in preferences or who illustrate confusion should be reassured through appropriate counseling and/or tutoring.

## LESSON PLAN FORM

| Goal | C1. Clarifying Occupational Self Concept |
|---|---|

Lesson Plan #   5          Grade Level   8

LESSON TITLE   Planning for Career Exploration

A. General Objective (unit theme)

  3.   Formulates tentative career hypotheses.

B. Specific Objectives(s)

  3.7  Prepares tentative career plan for occupational and educational exploration.

C. Instructional Materials, Supplies, and Equipment

  1.   Students' revised list of occupational preferences.

  2.   Optional teacher-developed activity sheets re step 2.1.

D. Unique Learner Needs or Characteristics

Three classes will complete this unit with a total enrollment of 58 (22-19-17). Males and females are approximately equally represented. All students are at least average in scholastic aptitude. However, about half of them are weak in verbal and writing skills.

All students have previously been introduced to the 15 occupational cluster areas. All students have used the *Occupational Outlook Handbook* at least once, but none extensively.

## LESSON PLAN FORM *(cont.)*

| Periods | Est. Time | |
|---|---|---|
| | | 1. *Preparation Step* |
| | 2 min. | 1.1 Begin by recalling that in the previous lesson students collected specific types of information about their occupational preferences. Based on such information, it is likely that further clarification may have taken place. For example, a student may have learned that one of his or her prior aspirations requires working in a setting much different than originally thought. |
| | 3 min. | 1.2 Explain to students that their orientation to occupations and appraisal of self up to this point in their career has been primarily *verbal* and *mental.* That is, they essentially have only read about, thought about, and talked about their aspirations and preferences. |
| | 5 min. | 1.3 Point out that the purpose of the following lesson is to have them develop a *plan of action* for testing and trying out their occupational preferences. The so-called "career plan," which is the outcome of this lesson, need not be thought of as anything rigid or formal. Rather the purpose is simply for students to identify education and work activities which have the potential to afford opportunities for trying out and testing occupational preferences. |
| 1 | | 2. *Presentation Step* |
| | 30 min. | 2.1 Using a teacher-prepared activity sheet, or one that students develop themselves, ask students to identify the various ways they can test their occupational preferences with respect to the following categories: |
| | (complete as home-work) | a. *High school coursework.* Identify how required academic courses may relate to occupational preferences. If career education courses are offered, what particular clusters are available for exploring? What |

## LESSON PLAN FORM *(cont.)*

| Periods | Est. Time | |
|---------|-----------|---|
| | | elective courses might contribute to the testing of preferences? |
| | | b. *Extra curricular activities.* What clubs and related organizations are available? Possible responses might include Journalism Clubs, Vocational Youth Groups (DECA, VICA, FFA, etc.), Future Teachers, etc. |
| | | c. *Non-school groups and organizations.* Many civic and business groups sponsor organizations which relate to career exploration. For example, the Explorer Scout Program, Junior Achievement, and church-sponsored career education activities. |
| | | d. *Work experience.* Both paid and unpaid work experiences are obviously one of the most realistic ways to test occupational interests, abilities and values. |
| | | 2.2 When all students have identified several examples related to the above four categories this step should be concluded. |
| | optional | 2.3 Depending on available time and the extent of personnel resources in the community, a wide variety of individuals can be invited into the classroom to assist in the identification and discussion of opportunities for career exploration. Similarly, students could be expected to do a great deal on their own in researching and interviewing toward achieving the objective of this lesson. |
| | | 3. *Application Step* |
| | 10 min. | 3.1 An important outcome associated with this lesson should be the realization that trial and testing is to be preferred over less active approaches in formulating educational and occupational preferences. The instructor might illustrate the differences among a *passive role* (reading or thinking about), a *simulated role* (say a classroom-operated selling enterprise), |

## LESSON PLAN FORM *(cont.)*

| Periods | Est. Time | |
|---|---|---|
| 2 | | and an *experiential role* (delivering newspapers and going door-to-door making collections). |
| | 20 min. | 3.2 Call on students to provide examples related to each of these roles: passive, simulated, and experiential. |
| | 10 min. | 3.3 Students, of course, should be made aware that because of their age and because of education and training requirements of many occupations they may be unable to truly experience some occupations. For example, being a "Candy Striper" in a hospital is not the same as being an RN in charge of a surgical unit. On the other hand, "Working as a Candy Striper" and being able to experience the environment in a hospital is infinitely more realistic than reading a book about nurses. |
| | | 4. *Evaluation Step* |
| 3 | variable | 4.1 Feedback for this lesson should consist of the student sharing and discussing his or her career objectives with parents and/or other adults (some of whom should be individuals working at the student's preferred occupation). Such consultation and advice from adults should help to provide additional assistance to the student in identifying objectives for career exploration. |
| | | 4.2 Students' career plans should be collected and filed with other materials from this unit for later use in actually planning and enrolling in a high school curriculum. |

# INDEX

## AUTHOR INDEX